Sew Much Fleece

Sew Much Fleece

20 Fun, Fast, and Fabulous Projects for the Whole Family

COMPILED BY
Karen M. Burns

Martingale®
Create with Confidence

Sew Much Fleece: 20 Fun, Fast, and Fabulous Projects for the Whole Family

Martingale®
19021 120th Ave. NE, Ste. 102
Bothell, WA 98011-9511 USA
ShopMartingale.com

Printed in China
20 19 18 17 16 15 8 7 6 5 4 3 2 1

Library of Congress Cataloging-in-Publication Data is available upon request.

ISBN: 978-1-60468-711-8

Mission Statement

Dedicated to providing quality products and service to inspire creativity.

Credits

PUBLISHER AND CHIEF VISIONARY OFFICER
Jennifer Erbe Keltner

EDITORIAL DIRECTOR
Karen Costello Soltys

MANAGING EDITOR
Tina Cook

ACQUISITIONS EDITOR
Karen M. Burns

TECHNICAL EDITOR
Laurie Baker

COPY EDITOR
Melissa Bryan

DESIGN DIRECTOR
Paula Schlosser

PHOTOGRAPHER
Brent Kane

PRODUCTION MANAGER
Regina Girard

COVER AND INTERIOR DESIGNER
Connor Chin

ILLUSTRATOR
Missy Shepler

Contents

Page 20

Page 47

Page 59

Introduction

Move over, denim. Fleece may now be America's favorite fabric—and what's not to love? This soft, snuggly fabric is lightweight, easy to care for, and doesn't shrink, ravel, or fray, so no seam finishing is needed. Available in 60" widths in fun prints and solids that don't fade, fleece is an affordable option for both wearables and home-decor sewing. But what, exactly, *is* it?

Fleece is a blanket term (pun intended) for a knit fabric that has a brushed finish on one or both sides. While most fleece is polyester, some fleece is made from recycled plastic soda and water bottles or new man-made fibers. There's even organic fleece, made from cotton and bamboo! High-end fleece, used in serious outdoor gear, is manufactured for water and wind repellency or antimicrobial properties.

Fleece is available in different weights, from light to heavy, and in a variety of textures. Some fleece is printed with one-way designs (for example, standing deer or upright flowers), so consider that as you shop; in some instances, a project may require more fabric to accommodate the directional print.

Don't Get Balled Up

Pilling is the development of little balls of fiber on the fabric surface. Some fleeces are prone to this unsightly trait because they're made from shorter fibers that tend to pill more with wear and abrasion. If you're put off by pilling, look for "anti-pill" on the end of the bolt to select fabrics that minimize this characteristic.

Don't worry that you need to know all about fleece. The projects in this book don't require a degree in fleece-ology. Just visit your local fabric store, find a fleece (or three!) that you love, and then dive in.

You'll find that the projects are designed to let you have fun with fleece. They're fast and pretty easy to sew for yourself, family members, and your favorite pet companions. Plus, you'll find little or no fitting involved in sewing these items, which makes them ideal for gift giving.

Look for the "Just a Thought . . ." informational tidbits throughout that can extend the idea of the basic project, either with some creative embellishments or other ideas for personalizing.

So get ready, get set, and sew up some fun fleece projects!

Tools of the Trade

This section will cover the basic tools you need for working with fleece (What You'll Need), along with notions that aren't required but *do* make sewing with fleece easier (What You'll Want).

What You'll Need

The great thing about fleece is that you don't need a lot of special tools to work with it, and you probably already have most of the necessities in your sewing arsenal.

Because fleece is bulky, it's a good idea to use **long pins** with a sturdy shaft and sizable heads on them, so they can easily go through two layers without bending and still be visible. Look for fun pins with ball heads, or novelty heads like flowers or buttons. Having a colorful pin head will help you easily see and pull out the pins before you get to them while sewing seams.

Cutting fleece is easy with a **rotary cutter, mat, and ruler.** With these items, you can achieve a clean, straight cut edge on even the bulkiest of fleeces. For most projects, using a rotary cutter is easier than cutting with scissors. Use a 60 mm rotary cutter for heavier fleeces and multiple layers and a 45 mm cutter for lighter weights and single layers. Because fleece consists of man-made fibers, it's hard on both scissors and rotary-cutter blades, so be sure to carefully wipe off accumulated lint as you cut, and have extra blades on hand. If you prefer to use **scissors,** sharp scissors are a must, and those with serrated blades are even better for cutting through the fleecy bulk.

Pattern weights are helpful for holding pattern pieces in place while cutting fleece. If you don't have any weights, consider purchasing large metal washers at the hardware store, or head to the silverware drawer in your kitchen to gather some knives, forks, and spoons.

A colorful **chalk marker** will help you denote the fabric wrong side. Chalk pencils, squares or triangles, and roller applicators are all good options.

Best NOT to Press

One tool that you really *don't* need is an iron, because it's easy to imprint the fabric and ruin your project. If you're a compulsive presser, go ahead and use an iron, but hover it above the area you're pressing—never touch the fleece. Not only can ironing crush the surface, but the fibers could actually melt or scorch. For 99% of seaming and detailing, finger-pressing works just fine.

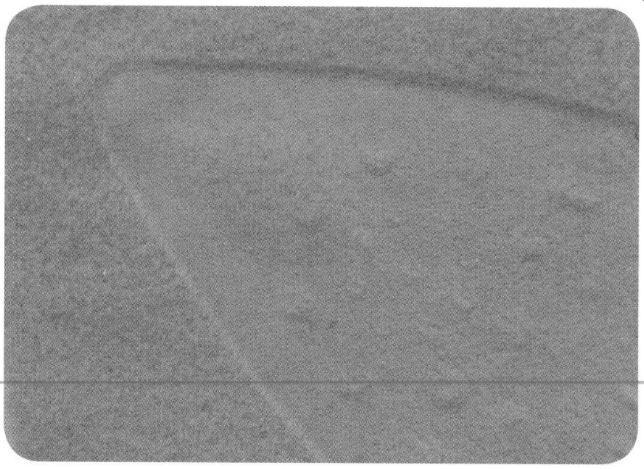

Fleece is easily overpressed!

To prevent skipped stitches while seaming, opt for a **ballpoint or jersey needle** in a size compatible with the fleece weight. A size 11/75 or 80/12 is a good choice for lightweight fleeces, while a 14/90 works well for heavier varieties. A ballpoint needle goes between the fibers of the fleece's knit base without piercing them and causing damage like a sharp-point needle can. If you're using a thread that's heavier than all-purpose thread, choose a size 16/100 needle or a topstitching needle, which has a larger eye to accommodate the thread weight.

A **chenille needle,** with its sharp point and large eye, is beneficial for hand stitching embellishments in place with heavy threads such as pearl cotton.

A **walking foot** can be helpful when sewing seams. Multiple layers of bulky fleece can sometimes shift under the foot, causing the layers to misalign or the edges to stretch; a walking foot keeps all the layers feeding evenly at the same speed. If you don't have a walking foot, lighten the presser-foot pressure to help prevent rippling when seaming. Some walking feet have an attached quilting guide for evenly spaced stitching lines, which comes in handy when sewing multiple rows of parallel stitching.

A **point turner** or **ballpoint bodkin** can be useful for pushing out the points in tight corners or narrow seams.

What You'll Want

Many companies have developed notions that work especially well with fleece fabrics. They're not a requirement, but they can make your project sew up a little easier.

There's nothing like a little spritz of adhesive to hold something in place while you stitch it. **Temporary spray adhesive** can be just the thing for that purpose. It's perfect for positioning the *W-O-O-F* letters on the "Comfy Pet Perch" (page 56). If you don't get the shapes in the right place, just lift and reposition. Temporary spray adhesive dissipates over time, so there's no messy residue left in your project. Just spritz, sew, and go!

Another aid for keeping things in place is **fleece glue.** It's permanent and washable, so if you don't want to attach a fleece accent with stitching,

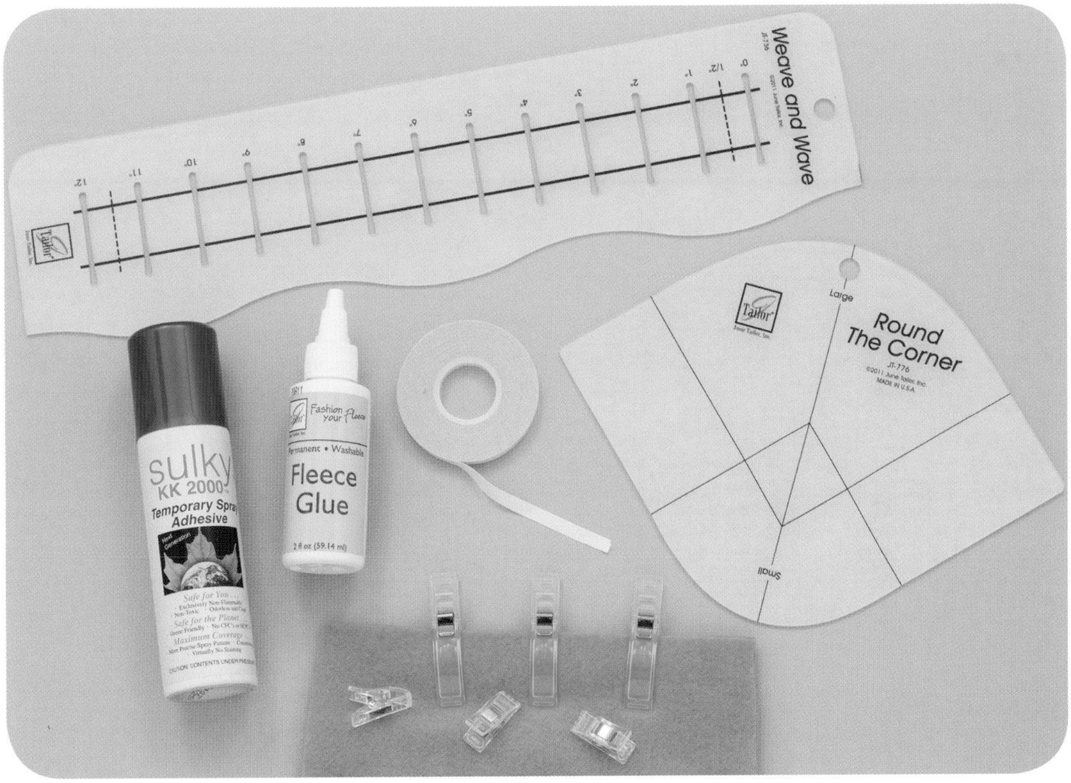

What you'll *want* for fleece sewing are some specialized notions to make the job easier.

just glue it in place. It's also great for kids to use because there's no needle, thread, or scissors involved.

Keep layers from shifting while sewing using ¼"-wide, water-soluble **basting tape.** It's almost a must-have notion when inserting a zipper (such as in the "Zippered Cowls" on page 23). It also works well for temporarily securing hems and turned-back edges while you permanently stitch them in place.

Fleece is bulky, no doubt about it. Tame those thick layers and bulky hems with **clips.** Like old-fashioned spring clothespins only in modern-day colorful plastic, these handy helpers are available in different sizes and hold things firmly in place for stitching. Choose a clip specifically designed for use on fabric to avoid marring the fleece surface.

Specialty rulers can be handy for many fleece-cutting tasks. Look for a slotted ruler for accurately and evenly cutting fringe strips (on the "Comfy Pet Perch and Toy" on page 56, for example) and a rounded corner ruler for rounding corners (like on the "Ruffly Shoulder Wrap" on page 31).

If you're giving your fleece project hand-stitched details, such as a blanket-stitched edge, it can be difficult to space stitches evenly. **Tiger Tape** is a narrow, adhesive-backed tape with equally spaced markings along the length. Each mark shows you where to insert the needle for the next stitch, enabling you to achieve precise spacing. When you're done with the stitching, simply pull the tape off—there's no residue or fabric damage.

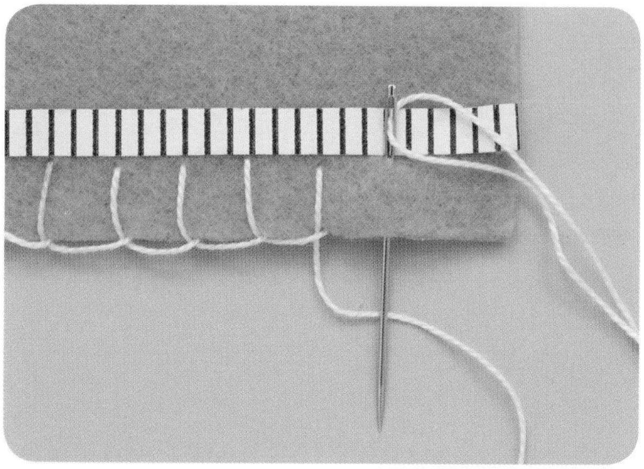

Here, we used Tiger Tape and aligned stitches with every third line for evenly spaced blanket stitches.

Die Cutters

A die cutter consists of a shaped metal die with a very sharp edge that can cut through multiple layers of fabric without effort, producing identical shapes over and over. While it's handy for cutting appliqué and patchwork shapes, it can also greatly simplify cutting small fleece shapes and accents that are tricky to mark and tend to be squirmy on the cutting surface. Simply follow the manufacturer's instructions to load the fleece into the machine and turn the handle (or turn on the machine if it's electric), and voilà—perfect shapes! Look for the special icon throughout the book that indicates projects that lend themselves well to the use of die cutters.

Die-cutter friendly!

Getting Started

Using the right cutting and sewing techniques will make sewing fleece as easy as can be. Let's look at some basics before you get going.

Cutting

Because fleece has a surface texture (commonly known as "nap"), all the pieces of a project need to be cut in the same direction to avoid shading (one part appearing lighter or darker than another) in the finished item. This means the lower edge of all pattern pieces must point in the same direction. If you follow this rule, you'll have no trouble with directional prints either. Nothing is worse than finding out that half of your project has deer standing on their heads, while the other half has them on their feet.

Before you start cutting out your project pieces, choose which side of the fleece you want to use as the right side. If it's a print, the pattern may be more distinct on one side than the other, so the decision is a no-brainer. On solids, it's a little trickier. Look at the fleece along a cut edge and see which side has the thicker pile—that's the right side. Often, though, there's not a lot of difference. Some people believe that if you pull a swatch of fleece on the crosswise grain, it will curl to the wrong side; others swear it curls to the right side. Truth be told, it's up to you—pick one side you like and use it consistently throughout your project.

Can you tell the right side of the fleece from the wrong side?

Unless the fleece is a heavy weight, you can usually cut through two layers at once. If the fleece seems too bulky to double, cut through a single layer instead. Make sure that if the shape is asymmetrical and you need two pieces (such as for the front and back of the "Hand Warmers" on page 26), you flip the pattern piece over to cut the second piece.

Marking

Transferring markings to fleece can be done in several ways. A contrasting-color chalk works well for most markings, like dots for matching, fold lines, and hemlines. A sliver of soap works equally well for fine-line marking.

As another marking option, use small stickers that simply adhere to the wrong side of the fleece, and then peel them off when the mark is no longer needed.

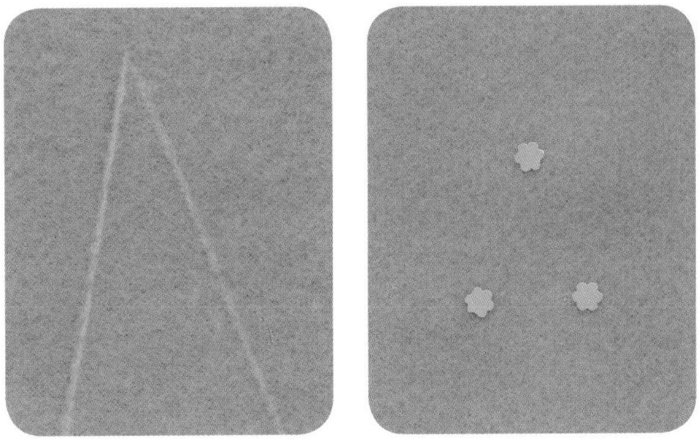

Chalk (left) and stickers (right) are two options for marking fleece.

Seaming

All-purpose polyester sewing thread is a good choice for fleece seaming. Like fleece itself, polyester sewing thread stretches, and it comes in a wide range of colors to match any fleece. Note that because the stitches sink into the fleece pile, an exact color match isn't necessary, but the stitches can also be difficult to remove if you make a mistake, so stitch slowly and carefully. Backstitch at the beginning and end of any seams that won't be crossed by another line of stitching, or tie the thread ends to secure them.

You have several stitch options for sewing fleece (specifics to follow). No matter which stitch you use, if you have trouble with your fleece slipping while sewing, a walking foot will help prevent the movement. The foot has teeth underneath its surface to help move both layers along at the same pace for even feeding.

Depending on the project, seams can be inside the garment or other item as they are for traditional sewing, or they can be exposed (visible on the project exterior) for a decorative effect. If you put the seam allowances on the outside, consider trimming them with a decorative-edge rotary blade or ruler.

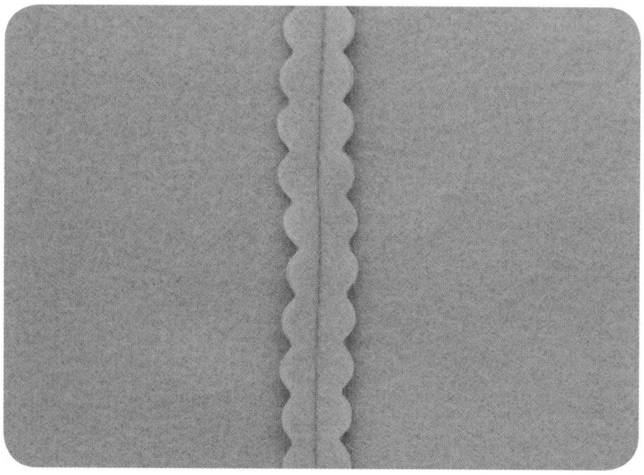

Exposed seams can be trimmed using a specialty rotary-cutter blade or scissors.

Straight Stitch

Most fleece seams can be sewn with a simple straight stitch. Choose a length slightly longer than used for other sewing tasks—a 3.5 mm stitch length is ideal for most fleece seaming. Note that a straight-stitch seam should be used only in an area that doesn't require stretch and flexibility.

A straight stitch is ideal for sewing fleece.

Zigzag

A narrow, open zigzag stitch (2.0 mm width, 2.0 mm length) is ideal for seaming fleece and provides stretch where needed.

Zigzag stitches stretch with the fleece.

Overcast Stitch

Some machines offer a built-in overcast stitch, also known as an overedge stitch, that sews a straight-seam portion and a zigzag variation at the same time. With built-in stretch, this is another stitch that's ideal for seaming fleece.

An overcast stitch also stretches with the fleece.

Serging

Sewing fleece seams with a serger is the fastest and easiest of all the methods, because the seam is stitched and trimmed at the same time. The encased serged edge also helps to flatten the seam allowance. If your serger is equipped with differential feed, engaging the feature can help prevent seams from stretching or rippling.

Sew and trim your seams at the same time by using a serger.

Topstitching

One way to flatten seams and keep them where you want them is to topstitch them after sewing. Seams can be finger-pressed to one side and topstitched, or, for a wider seam, they may be opened and topstitched on both sides.

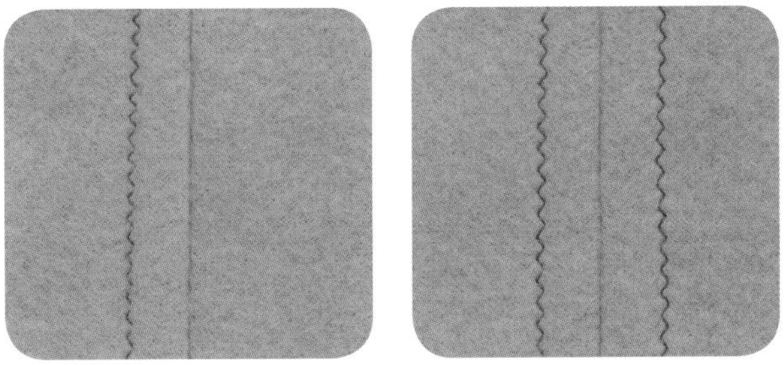

Topstitch seams to keep them flat.

For topstitching, investigate twin needles for a professional look. A twin needle is two needles on a single shank used to create a double row of parallel stitches. The underside of the stitching is a zigzag (maintaining some stretch) because there's only a single bobbin to span the double row of stitches. Twin needles come in various widths, from 1.6 mm to 9 mm tip to tip. Check your owner's manual for the maximum-width needle your sewing machine can accommodate.

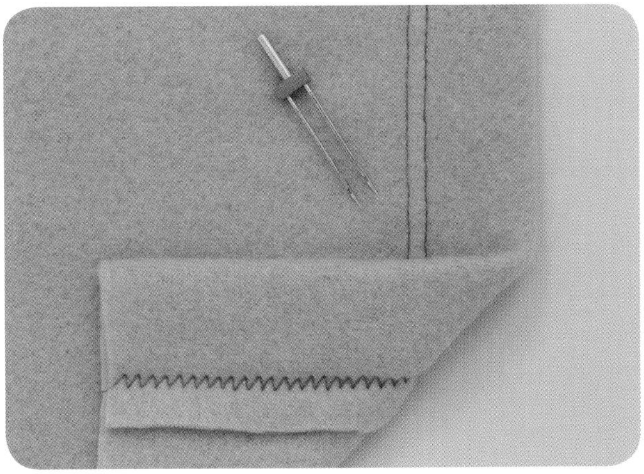

Create a double row of topstitching with a twin needle.

Hemming

The beauty of fleece is that no edge finishing is needed, so a traditional turned-under hem isn't required. If you prefer a turned-under finish, pin or clip the hem in place, and add one or more rows of topstitching. Stitching with a double needle creates a professional-looking finish and creates two exactly parallel rows in one pass.

Finishing the Edges

The no-ravel character of fleece allows for some creative edge finishes using novelty rotary-cutter blades and/or scissors. Look for scalloped, pinking, and wave blades to use for simple cut-edge finishes.

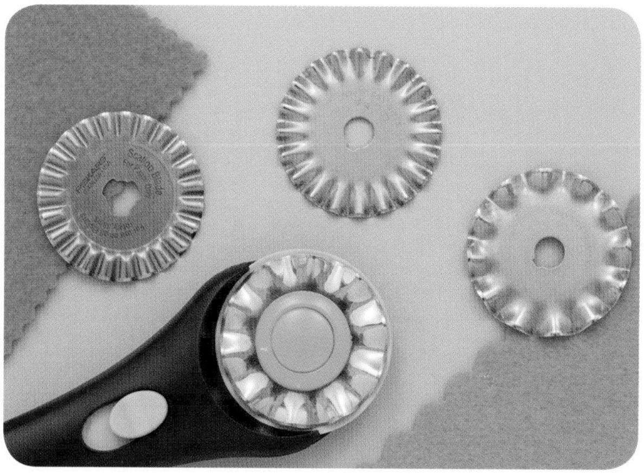

Novelty rotary-cutter blades are available to create a variety of decorative edge finishes.

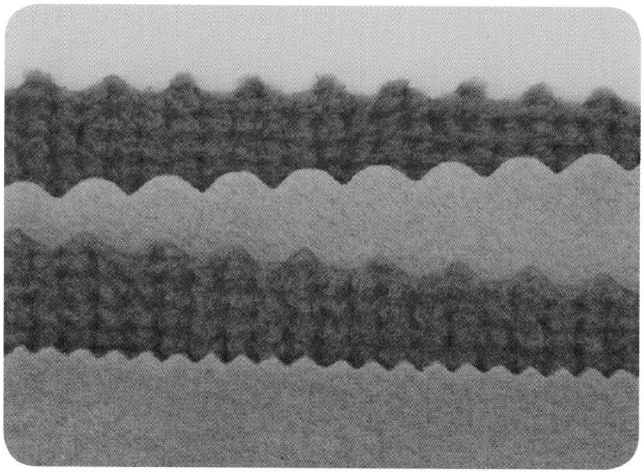

Create waves, scallops, zigzags, and more with novelty blades.

Also check out perforating rotary-cutter blades that cut evenly spaced slits, perfect for threading ribbon, blanket stitching, or adding a lacing or crocheted edge.

Make evenly spaced cuts with a perforating blade.

Serging can also be used as an edge finish on its own, either with matching threads for an unobtrusive look or with decorative threads as a colorful accent.

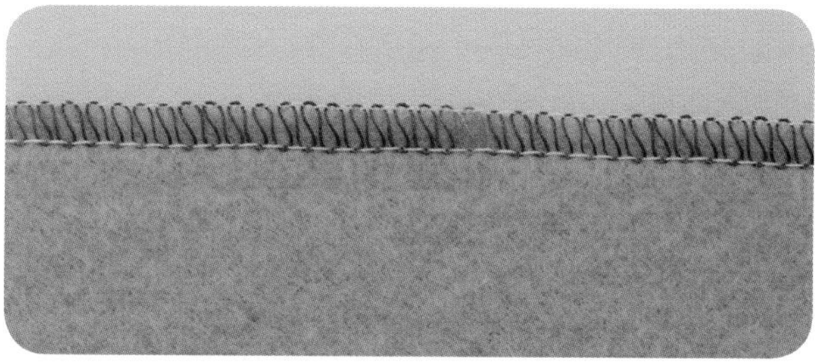

Finish edges with serging.

A rolled edge adds a textural option to an exposed seam. After stitching the seam, roll the upper ½" seam allowance toward the top layer, tucking the cut edge of the seam allowance within the roll. Slip-stitch the rolled edge to the top layer to secure it. To make a double-rolled edge, roll the remaining ½" seam allowance toward the first rolled edge, and slipstitch it in place to secure it.

Add texture with a rolled edge.

Ruffled, or "lettuce," edging is easy to add because the stretchiness of fleece actually facilitates the process. Set your sewing machine to a dense, wide zigzag (0.3 mm length, 6.0 mm width). Holding the fabric edge behind and in front of the presser foot, stretch the fleece while sewing over the cut edge.

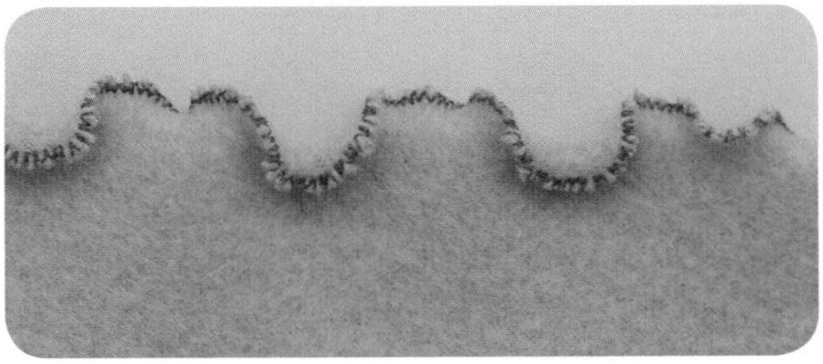

Stretch the fabric while sewing to create a ruffled edge.

Try a decorative stitch on your machine to finish an edge. Look for stitches formed with only a forward motion; stitches created with a reverse-cycle pattern are often problematic on bulky fleece and can cause distortion.

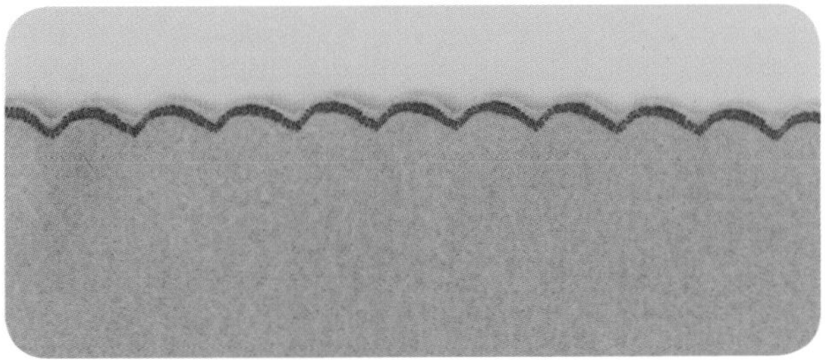

Trim close to a decoratively stitched edge.

Decorative stitching can also be used for seam accents, topstitching, hemming, or simply adding interest to a project or section of a garment. Remember that the stitches will sink into the fleecy surface, creating a subtly textured effect.

Twin-Needle Tricks

Tightening the tension when using twin needles can create a raised ridge between the stitching lines. When repeated across an area, this can look like ribbing. Depending on the needle spacing, tension, and fleece weight, the raised area(s) can be very prominent or ever so subtle. Test-sew and play on fleece scraps to see what you can create.

Straight lines of twin-needle stitching mimic the look of ribbing.

Double-needle stitching can also be used in a free-form manner to create design areas across an otherwise flat section of fleece.

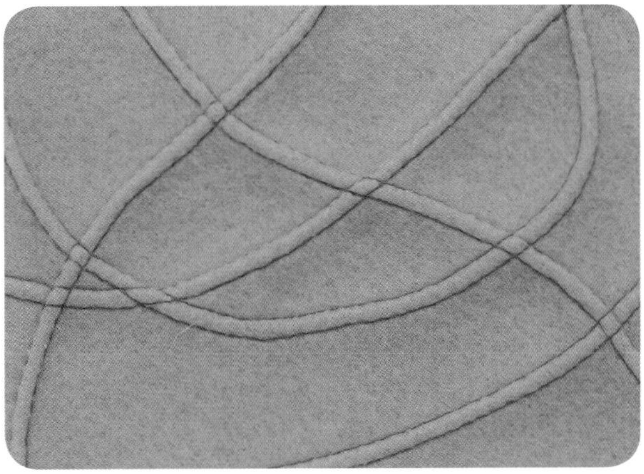

Create interest and texture with free-form twin-needle stitching.

Going to Great Lengths Hats

by Linda Turner Griepentrog

Sizes: S, M, L to fit 21", 22", and 23" head circumferences

Just a single yard of fleece yields three different versions of this fun stocking cap with assorted details and matching pom-pom trim.

Make three hats from just one yard of fleece.

Materials (for 3 hats)

Yardage is based on 60"-wide fabric.

1 yard of black-and-white polka-dot fleece for hats

¼ yard of red solid fleece for pompoms and trims

3" x 3" square of green solid fleece for leaves

4 mm twin needle

Hand-sewing needle

Chalk marker

Pattern-tracing material

Making the Front/Back Hat Pattern

Draw a 12½" x 34¼" rectangle onto pattern-tracing material. Measure in 5¼" from each side along the top edge. Draw a line from each mark to the corresponding bottom corner as shown. Mark the stretch-direction arrow parallel to the bottom edge. Cut out the pattern on the drawn lines.

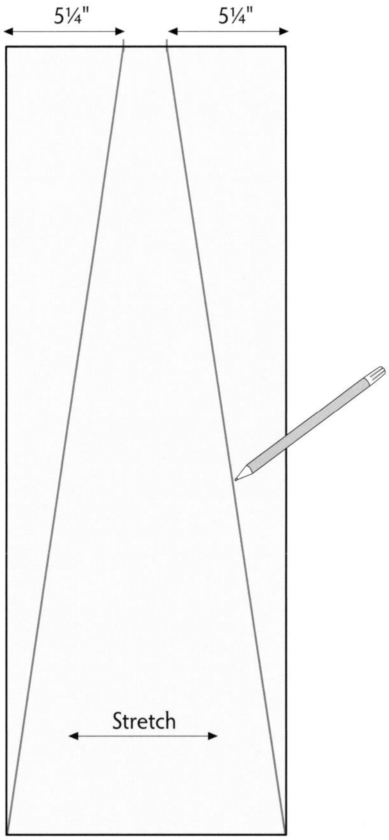

Just a Thought . . .

- Sew a pin back to the flower so you can wear it on other garments. Add more folded circles if you want a larger bloom.
- Mix and match the colors used in the hat—cut the front from one color and the back from another. It's a great way to use up scraps or make something in school colors.
- Instead of a pom-pom, top this hat with a large jingle bell for holiday fun. Use a narrow strip of fleece to attach the bell to the hat tip.

Cutting

Remove the selvages from the fabrics before cutting. To cut all 3 hats from 1 yard of fleece, alternate the direction of the second hat, keeping the fabric stretch going around the head. The circle and leaf patterns are on page 19.

From the red solid fleece, cut:

3 strips, 3" x 24"

3 strips, 1" x 8"

20 circles

From the black-and-white fleece, cut:

3 sets of front/back hat pieces (keep each set together as cut)

From the green solid fleece, cut:

2 leaves

Making the Pom-Poms

1. Lay out a red 3" x 24" strip on a flat surface. Chalk-mark a line along the lengthwise center.

2. Carefully cut into the strip every ¼" to ½" along both sides, leaving ¼" intact through the lengthwise center.

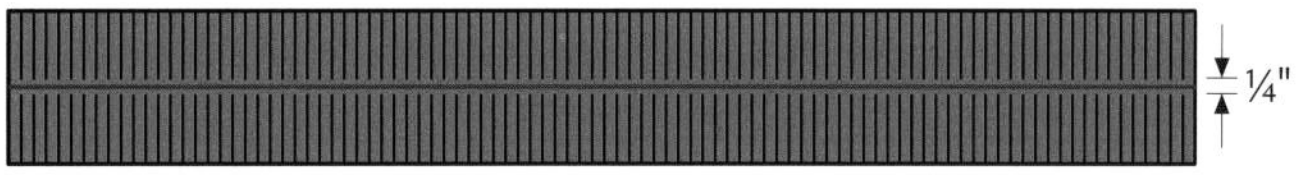

3. Tightly roll up the slashed strip, being careful not to distort or fold the cut fringe.

4. Tie the red 1" x 8" strip around the fringe center as tightly as you can. Fluff the resulting pom-pom.

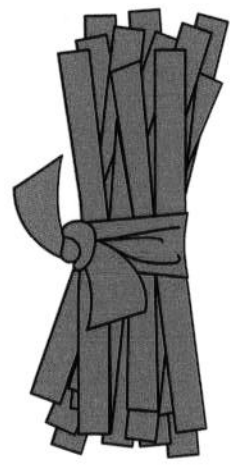

5. Repeat steps 1–4 to make a total of three pom-poms.

Making the Twin-Needle Hemmed Hat

1. Place one set of hat front/back pieces right sides together. Sew along the sides and across the narrow top end using a 1"-wide seam allowance for size small, a ¾"-wide seam allowance for size medium, and a ½"-wide seam allowance for size large. If sewn on a conventional machine, trim the seam allowances to ¼" wide.

2. Fold up the lower hem 1½" and pin or clip it in place. Insert the twin needle in the machine and stitch the hem in place 1" from the fold. Stitch again ¼" from the fold, and then sew a third row of stitching between the two previous lines of double stitching.

3. Turn the hat right side out. Sew a pompom to the hat tip either by hand or by machine; use the ends of the tie strip for attachment. Trim the extending tie ends.

Making the Flower-Trimmed Hat

Die-cutter friendly!

1. Repeat step 1 of the instructions for the twin-needle hemmed hat above to make the hat body.

2. Fold up the lower hem 2" and sew close to the cut hem edge using a small, narrow zigzag stitch (2.0 mm width, 2.0 mm length).

3. Turn the hat right side out. Fold up the bottom edge to cover the hem stitching line (slightly more than 1") and create a cuff.

4. Fold five red circles in half, and then fold them in half again; pin to hold the layers together. Using a doubled thread and the hand-sewing needle, stitch through the folded corner of each circle, lining them up the length of the thread.

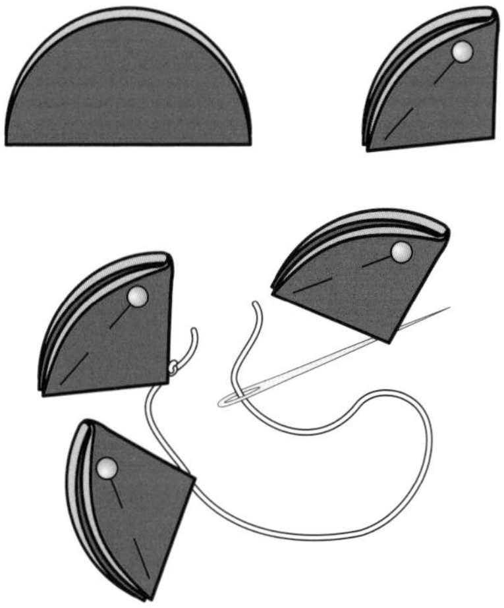

5. Pull the thread tightly to shape the circles into a flower and stitch the circles together several times at the corners. Open some of the circles to make the "bloom." Tie off the threads securely.

6. Fold each leaf in half lengthwise, and then place them side by side. Hand stitch the leaves together at the lower edges. Position the stitched end of the leaves under the flower and sew them in place.

7. Hand stitch the flower to the outside of the hat cuff.

8. If desired, hand tack the cuff in place from the wrong side.

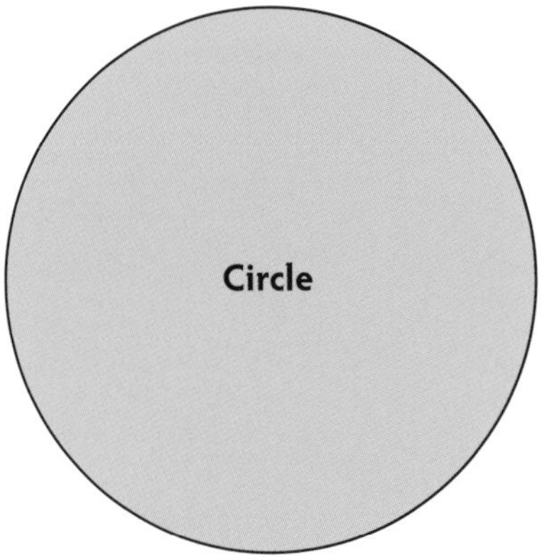

Making the Circle-Trimmed Hat

Die-cutter friendly!

1. Repeat step 1 of the instructions for the twin-needle hemmed hat on page 18 to make the hat body.

2. Chalk-mark a line along the lower portion of the hat's right side, 3½" from the raw edge.

3. Arrange the remaining 15 red circles around the hat's lower edge, overlapping the circles approximately ¼" and aligning the top edge of each circle with the marked line.

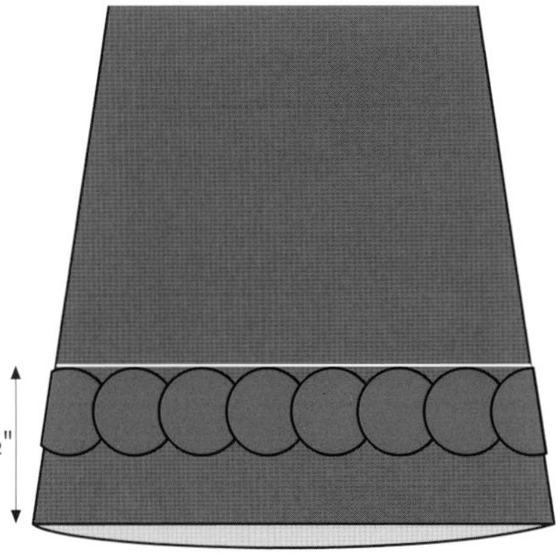

4. Stitch through the center of the circles 2½" from the hat's lower edge using a small, narrow zigzag stitch (2.0 mm width, 2.0 mm length).

5. Fold up the lower hem 2½" to the wrong side and sew close to the cut hem edge using a small, narrow zigzag stitch (2.0 mm width, 2.0 mm length).

6. Turn up the hat lower edge to create a cuff, leaving half of each circle extending above the folded edge. Hand tack the cuff in place or leave it free so you can wear the hat without a cuff as well, with circles highlighting the hem.

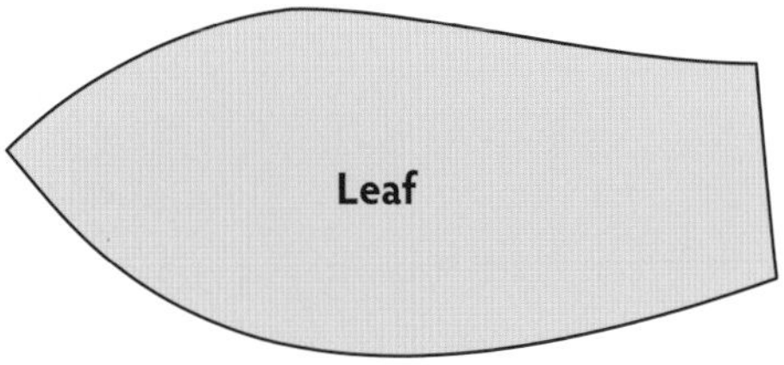

Sassy Scarf

by Linda Turner Griepentrog

Size: 6" x 48"

Whether you make it in one color or two, this fun scarf is simple to sew with just two lines of stitching and a little bit of elastic. It's a perfect venue to showcase decorative fleece edges on one or both layers.

Get the look of ruffles without the fuss!

Materials

Yardage is based on 60"-wide fabric.

⅜ yard of medium-blue fleece

⅜ yard of light-blue fleece

1¾ yards of ⅜"-wide elastic

Chalk marker

Large safety pin or bodkin

Temporary spray adhesive

Decorative rotary blade and cutter or decorative-blade scissors (optional)

Cutting

Remove the selvages from the fabrics before cutting.

From the medium-blue fleece, cut:

2 strips, 5½" x 40", using a decorative blade if desired

From the light-blue fleece, cut:

2 strips, 6" x 40"

From the elastic, cut:

1 piece, 48" long

Making the Scarf

1. Abut the short ends of the medium-blue strips and join them using a multiple zigzag stitch (5.0 mm width, 1.0 mm length). Repeat with the light-blue strips.

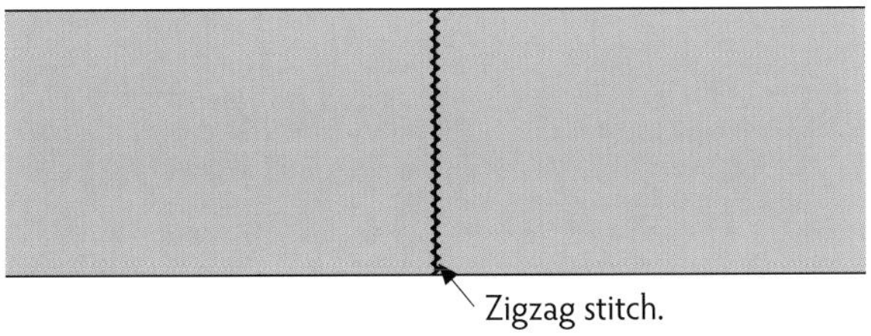

2. On the right side of the medium-blue strip, chalk-mark a line through the lengthwise center. Spray the wrong side of the strip with temporary adhesive.

Just a Thought . . .

- Use school colors for the scarf layers to showcase some spirit and keep warm at games.
- Sew a decorative stitch along the edge of one fleece layer as an embellishment. Trim the fleece close to the stitching.

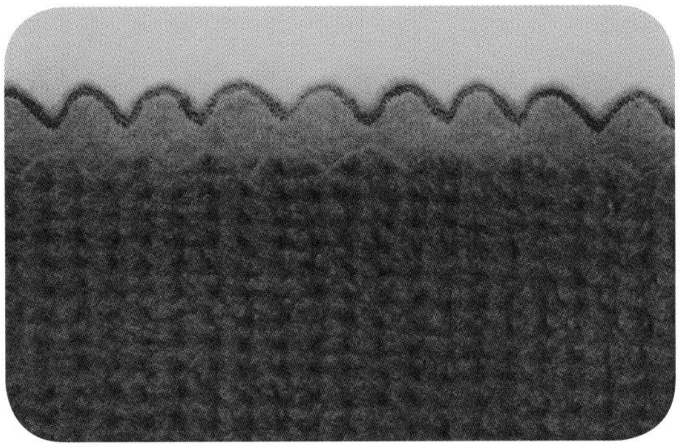

- "Lettuce" the edge of one scarf layer by zigzagging over the edge while stretching the fabric as much as possible.

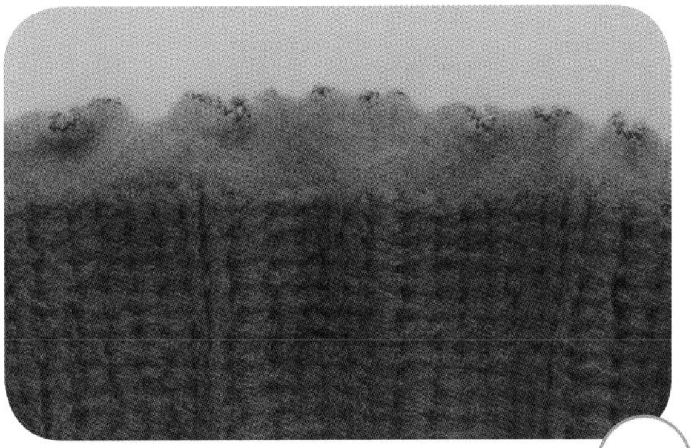

3. With right sides up, center the medium-blue strip over the light-blue strip and smooth it into place.

4. Stitch ¼" from each side of the marked line through both fleece layers to form a casing.

5. Using a safety pin or bodkin, thread the elastic through the casing, adjusting fullness evenly along the length. Stitch across the elastic at both ends twice to secure it, and trim any visible elastic at the ends.

6. Slightly round the scarf ends and trim them even, if desired.

Flower Power

Die-cutter friendly!

Add a fun, functional detail to your scarf with a dimensional flower that has a hidden elastic loop to hold the scarf ends together.

1. Using scraps from the scarf and the patterns below, cut one 4½", 3½", and 2½" circle *each* from one color of fleece and one 1½" circle from the contrasting color. Cut the edges with a decorative rotary-cutter blade or scissors for added interest.

2. Stack the circles in order from largest to smallest. Using a double thread, hand stitch a few soft pleats in the circle layers to form a flower shape.

3. Cut a 1" x 10" strip from the remainder of either of the fleece colors and a 10" length of ⅜"-wide elastic. Fold the fleece strip in half, wrong sides together, and zigzag stitch the long cut edges together. Using a safety pin or bodkin, thread the elastic through the tube and stitch across each end. Overlap the ends to form a circle, and then stitch the ends together.

4. Hand stitch the flower to the elasticized fleece loop over the joining seam.

5. Insert both ends of the scarf through the loop. Adjust as desired along the scarf length.

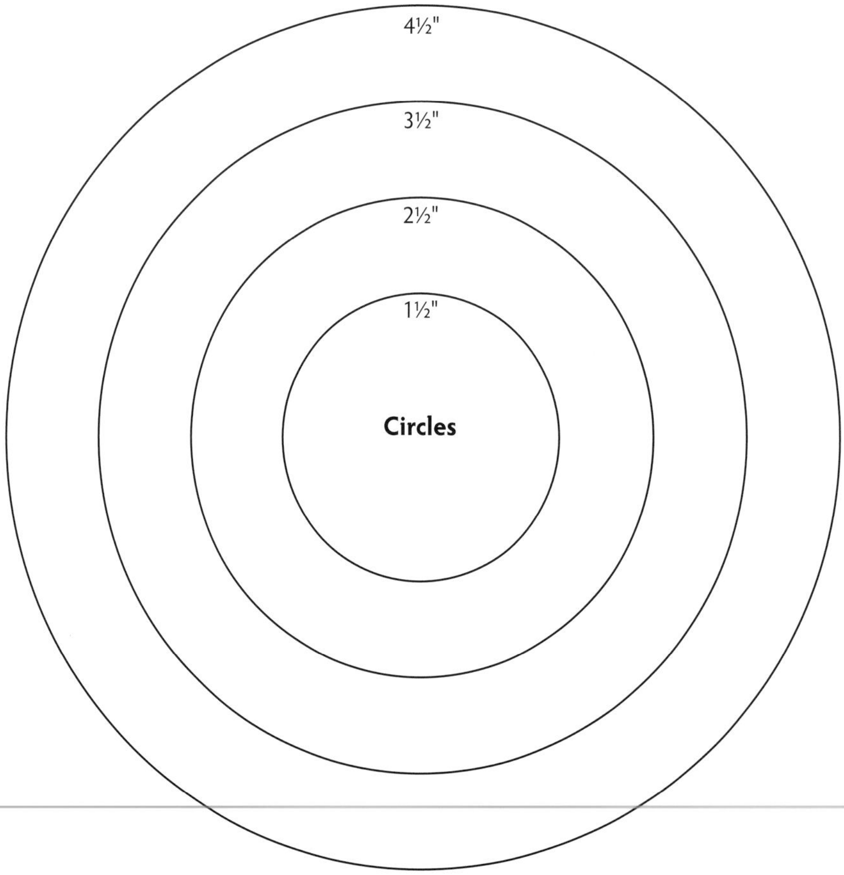

Zippered Cowls

by Missy Shepler
Sizes: 12" x 38" or 12" x 56"

Keep winter winds at bay in these fleecy fashions. Wear the short scarf zipped or partially open for a cowl-neck cuddler. Loop the long scarf twice around your neck and pull the top loop up for a hood, or unzip for standard scarf wear.

Short or long, each style has two ways to wear it.

Materials (for 1 scarf)

Yardage is based on 60"-wide fabric.

½ yard *each* of 1 print fleece and 1 coordinating-solid fleece

12"-long separating zipper

Seam sealant or clear fingernail polish

Cutting

Remove the selvages from the fabrics before cutting.

From *each* of the print and coordinating-solid fleeces, cut:

1 strip, 13" x 39", for short scarf *OR* 1 strip, 13" x 58", for long scarf

Assembling the Scarf

Use a ½"-wide seam allowance unless otherwise indicated.

1. Trim the upper end of the zipper tape even with the zipper stop. Dab the cut end of the zipper tape with a drop of seam sealant or clear fingernail polish to prevent the zipper tape from unraveling. Let the tape dry.

2. Place the cut rectangles right sides together, aligning the edges. Slip the zipper between the layered strips at one short end, making sure that the right side of the zipper faces the right side of the rectangle that you intend to wear as the outside of the scarf. Pin the zipper in place, making sure the ends of the zipper are ½" from the long edges of the rectangles.

3. Using a zipper foot and a ⅜" seam allowance, stitch along the pinned edge through all the layers. Start and stop stitching ½" from the long edges and catch the zipper tape in the seam.

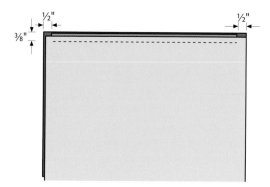

4. Repeat steps 2 and 3 to sew the remaining edge of the zipper tape to the opposite short ends of the strips. After pinning the zipper in place, unzip and separate the zipper to make stitching easier.

Just a Thought . . .

Add an infinity twist to your scarf! After topstitching the first edge of the zipper tape, place the scarf flat, with the outer side facing up. The rectangles should be wrong sides together. Grasp both unsewn short rectangle ends in one hand and turn them over so that the lining on that end is facing up. This introduces a single twist into the scarf. Follow assembly steps 2 and 3 to install the remaining edge of the zipper tape.

5. With the zipper unzipped and separated and the rectangles right sides together, pin each long edge together. Sew the long edges together along each side, leaving a 4" opening along one side for turning. Trim the seam allowances diagonally at each corner.

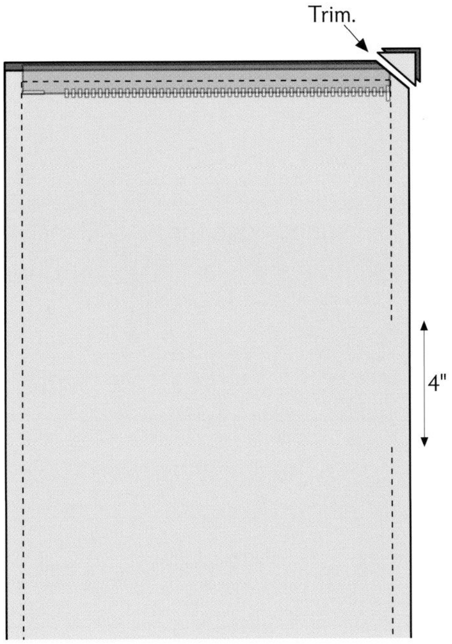

6. Turn the scarf right side out through the opening. Use a point turner to form a square corner at each zipper end. Check to make sure the zipper functions smoothly. Fold the seam allowances to the wrong side at the opening and pin the opening closed. Finger-press the seam along each side. Topstitch along each long edge, ¼" from the outer edge.

Adding Optional Details

If desired, add quilting lines and cutouts for extra texture and to keep long scarf layers together, as shown on the blue-plaid sample in the photo at right.

1. Place the scarf on a flat surface, smoothing out any folds or wrinkles. Pin the layers together to avoid shifting.

2. Using a chalk marker, draw four or five 2" squares on the scarf, positioning the squares as desired. Stitch around each square, just outside the marked lines.

3. Using a walking foot, topstitch several lines, 2½" apart, along the length of the scarf. Keep the stitching lines parallel to the long edges of the scarf, and start and stop ¼" from each short end. Do not stitch through the marked squares.

4. To make the cutouts, pull the fleece layers of a stitched square slightly apart. Using sharp scissors, make a clip in the lining layer of the scarf. Be careful not to cut through both layers. Trim only the lining fleece layer along the drawn square so that the outside fleece shows through the cut square. Repeat for the remaining squares.

Hand Warmers

by Missy Shepler

Size: Custom sized to your hand!

Make your own pattern for these fingerless mitts to get a perfect fit and the exact amount of coverage you want! Dress up your hand warmers with extra textures and fun appliqués.

Get a custom fit with a pattern drawn from your hand.

Materials

Yardage is based on 60"-wide fabric.

¼ to ½ yard of fleece, based on desired length (depending on individual size, yardage may yield 2 pairs)

11" x 17" sheet of paper or pattern-tracing material

For Optional Leaf Appliqués

(See page 30.)

9" x 12" rectangle of contrasting fleece

For Optional Flower Detail

6" x 6" square of print fleece for flowers

Scraps of coordinating fleece for flower leaves

2 pin backs, 1" long

Making the Pattern

1. Place your hand, palm down with the thumb and fingers slightly spread, on the sheet of paper or pattern-tracing material. Use a pencil to loosely trace around your hand and forearm.

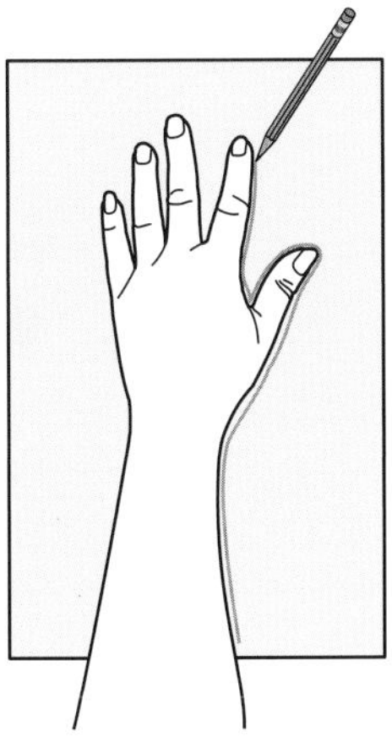

2. Use a measuring tape to measure the circumference of your hand around the knuckles, wrist, and the largest part of your forearm. Divide each measurement in half and compare the new numbers to the corresponding widths on the drawing. Mark the new widths on the drawing, on the side opposite the thumb. Draw a smooth curved line connecting the new marks. Determine the desired length of your hand warmers (should they cover your knuckles, extend to your elbows?), and draw lines to indicate those lengths.

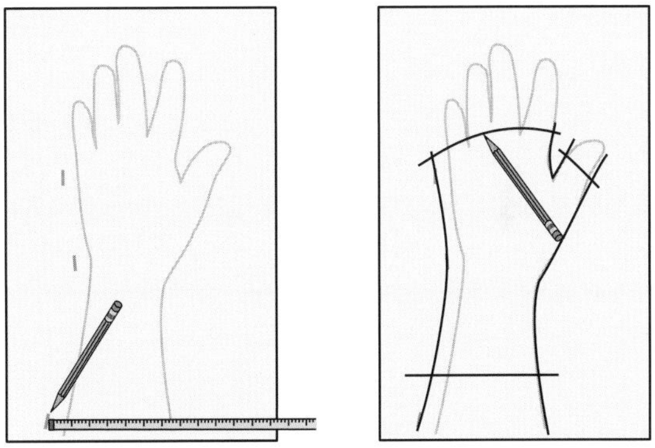

3. Add seam-allowance lines by drawing another line ½" outside the drawn line. This will be the cutting line. Draw an arrow at the base of the pattern parallel to the bottom edge to indicate

the direction the fabric should stretch. Cut out the pattern on the cutting lines.

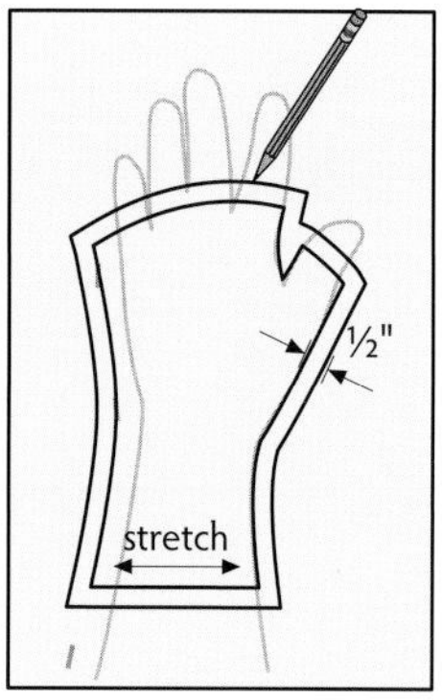

4. Flip the pattern over and lay it on the remainder of the paper or pattern-tracing material. Trace around the pattern to make a mirror-image hand warmer; cut out the pattern on the traced line. Mark the arrow at the bottom edge to indicate the direction the fabric should stretch.

Cutting the Pieces

Remove the selvages from the fabrics before cutting.

You have three options for adding texture to the hand warmers: ribbing, appliqués, or wavy edges with a three-dimensional flower detail. For the ribbed and appliquéd versions, you'll need to prepare the fabric before cutting out the pieces, using the paper patterns to roughly determine the placement of the details.

Ribbing

Narrow ribbing sewn parallel to the crosswise grain along the wrist edge creates a quick cuff effect (see the dark-gray hand warmers below). For a wider rib, take deeper seams.

1. Lay both patterns on one half of the fleece as shown, leaving twice the desired rib width *per rib* at the wrist end of the patterns. For example, for two ¼"-wide ribs, add 1" to the wrist end. Remove the patterns and roughly cut out two rectangles slightly larger than the determined size.

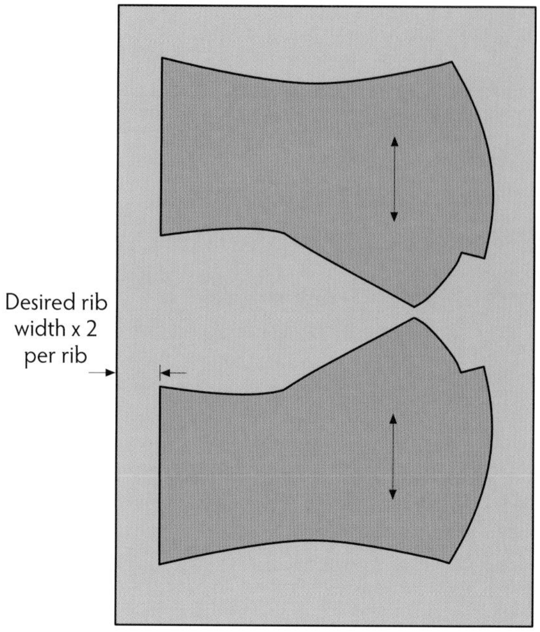

2. Fold one fleece rectangle wrong sides together at the wrist end of the fleece. For a narrow rib, stitch a seam parallel to and ⅛" to ¼" away from the fold. Unfold the fleece.

3. Repeat step 2 for each rib desired, folding the fleece wrong sides together ½" to ¾" from the previous line of stitching.

4. Repeat steps 2 and 3 with the remaining piece of fleece.

5. Place the pattern pieces on one of the ribbed fleece rectangles, with the ribs positioned at the same location on each hand warmer; pin in place through all the layers. Cut out the pieces. Repeat for the remaining fleece rectangle to cut the pieces for the second hand warmer. **Note:** It may be helpful to mark the position of the ribs on the pattern so that the ribs will align at the side edges.

6. Refer to "Assembling the Hand Warmers" on page 30 to complete the project.

Appliqué

Use an allover appliqué for an elegant effect, or create cuteness with a single element. Consider leaving the palms unadorned, because they'll rarely be seen, or add a single, secret element to hold in your hand. Add appliquéd leaves, shown on the light-gray hand warmers, as described below.

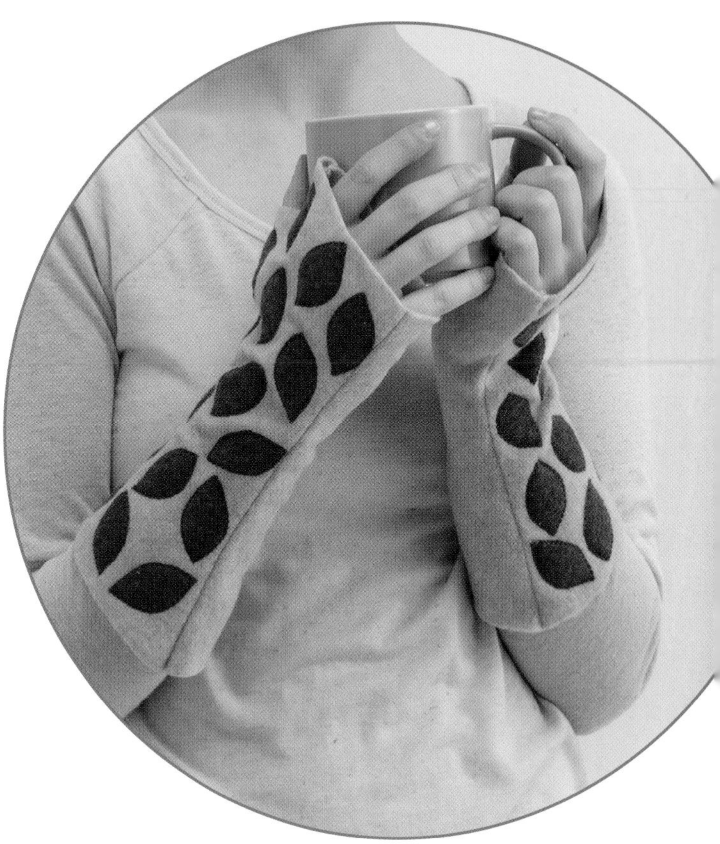

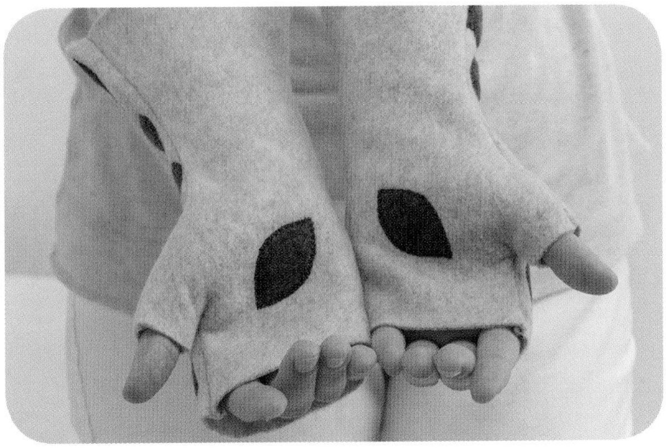

1. Lay the hand-warmer patterns on the right side of one half of the fleece as shown, and use a chalk marker to trace around them. Remove the patterns and then rough cut two rectangles 1" larger all around than the traced shapes.

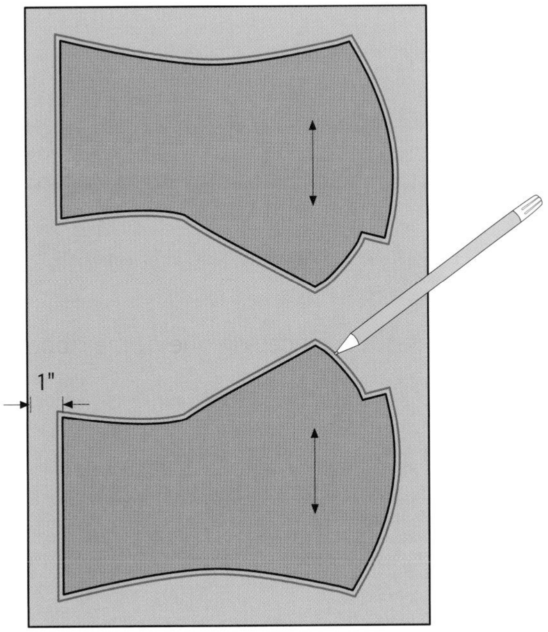

2. Using the leaf pattern on page 30, cut 34 leaves from the 9" x 12" contrasting fleece rectangle. Set aside two leaves for the palms.

3. Position 16 leaves within the lines of each traced hand-warmer shape on the marked fleece rectangle, placing the shapes at least ½" from the chalk lines so they won't be caught in the seam allowances. Pin the leaves in place.

4. Carefully stitch around the outer edge of each leaf on each hand warmer using a straight, zigzag, or decorative stitch of your choice. Sew slowly, taking care to secure the outer edges of each appliqué.

5. Use the patterns to cut one hand warmer and one reversed hand warmer from the plain fleece rectangle.

6. Center one of the remaining leaves on the right side of the palm of each plain fleece hand-warmer piece; stitch in place as before.

7. Refer to "Assembling the Hand Warmers" on page 30 to complete the project.

Just a Thought . . .

Instead of a leaf, appliqué a small heart to each palm of a pair of hand warmers, and give them to your sweetie on Valentine's Day.

Assembling the Hand Warmers

1. Place one hand warmer and one reversed hand warmer right sides together. For the ribbed version, be sure to match the ribs.

2. Using a ½" seam allowance for a close fit or a ¼" seam allowance for a slightly roomier fit, sew the two pieces together as shown, leaving the finger, thumb, and wrist openings open. Clip the seam allowances at the base of the thumb, being careful not to cut into the seam. Trim the seam allowances to ⅛".

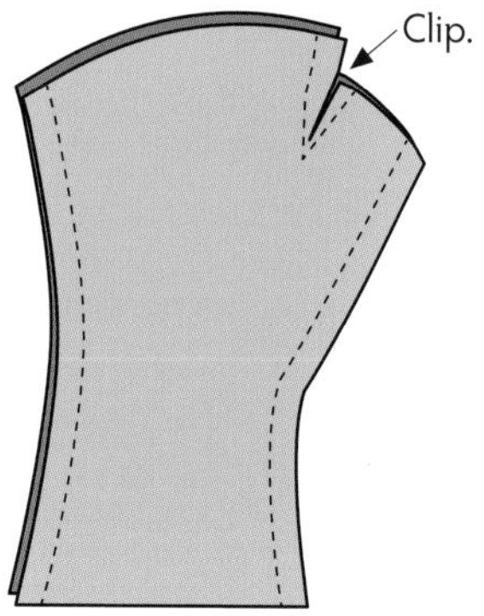

3. Turn the hand warmer right side out and finger-press the seam allowances.

4. Repeat steps 1–3 with the remaining pieces to make the opposite hand warmer.

Wavy Edges with Flower Detail

Decorative edging and a fun floral pin add interest to an otherwise plain-Jane hand warmer. To add edging as shown on the yellow mitts:

1. Using the patterns, cut two hand warmers and two reversed hand warmers from the fleece. Trim the finger, thumb, and wrist edges of each fleece piece using either a rotary cutter or scissors with a wave blade.

2. Using a decorative stitch, sew along the edges of the finger and thumb openings, ¼" from the deepest point of the wave.

3. Refer to "Assembling the Hand Warmers" at right to finish constructing the hand warmers.

4. Using the petal and leaf patterns below, cut 10 circles from the print 6" x 6" square and four leaves from the coordinating fleece scraps.

5. Follow steps 4–6 of "Making the Flower-Trimmed Hat" on page 18 to make two flowers; tack two leaves to the bottom of each flower.

6. Hand stitch a pin back to the bottom of each flower. Pin a flower to the cuff of each hand warmer.

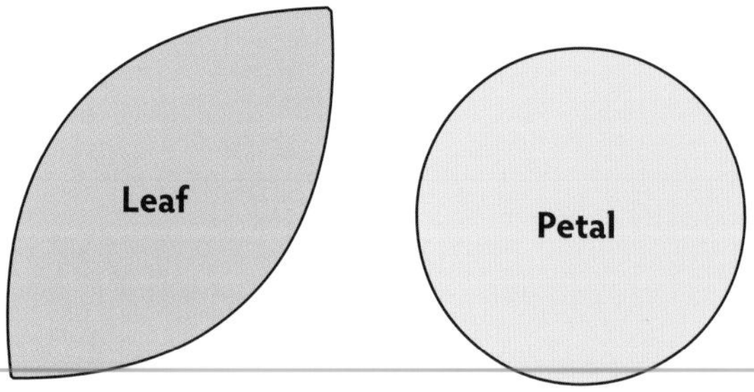

Ruffly Shoulder Wrap

by Linda Turner Griepentrog
Size: 20" x 59"

Perfect to take the chill off a cool evening out, this ruffled-edge shawl also makes a perfect gift—one size fits most.

Complete this frilly wrap in only an afternoon.

Materials

Yardage is based on 60"-wide fabric.

⅞ yard of print fleece

6" length of 1¾"-wide elastic

Hand-sewing needle

Cutting

Remove the selvages from the fabric before cutting.

From the print fleece, cut:

- 1 strip, 20" x 60"
- 1 rectangle, 3¾" x 6"
- 1 strip, 4½" x 13"
- 1 rectangle, 2" x 4"

Making the Shawl

1. Using a saucer or curved ruler, round the corners of the 20" x 60" strip.

2. Set the machine for a wide, close zigzag stitch (6.0 mm width, 0.3 mm length) and load a full bobbin. To create the ruffled edging, begin at the center back of the fleece strip and stitch over the fabric edge while stretching it to the maximum. When the fleece is released, it will form the ruffle. Stitch around the entire shawl in the same manner.

3. To make the tab, fold the 3¾" x 6" rectangle in half lengthwise, right sides together. Using a wide, open zigzag stitch (5.0 mm width, 3.0 mm length), sew the long edges together. Position the elastic on top of the stitched rectangle and zigzag stitch across one end. Turn the fleece tab right side out over the elastic, being careful not to twist the elastic. Zigzag stitch across the open end of the rectangle, catching the free end of the elastic in the stitching.

4. Stitch the unfinished end of the elasticized tab to the right side of the shawl as shown at right.

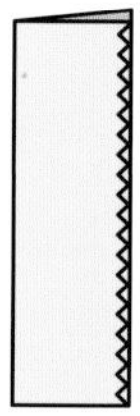

Zigzag stitch long edges together.

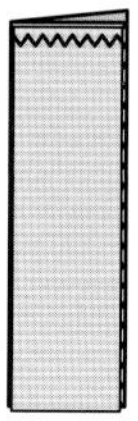

Zigzag stitch elastic to tab at one end.

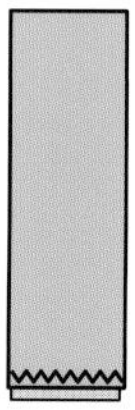

Turn tab right side out and zigzag stitch open end, catching elastic in stitching.

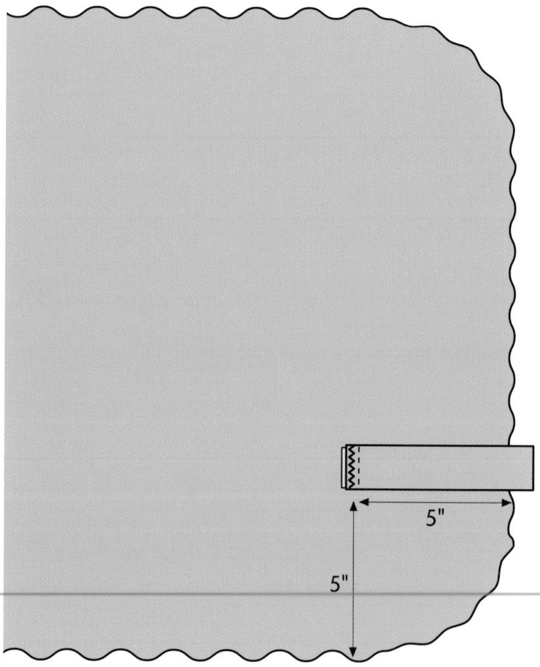

5. Hand stitch the finished tab end in place 5" from the unfinished tab end, noting that the tab will not lie flat against the shawl.

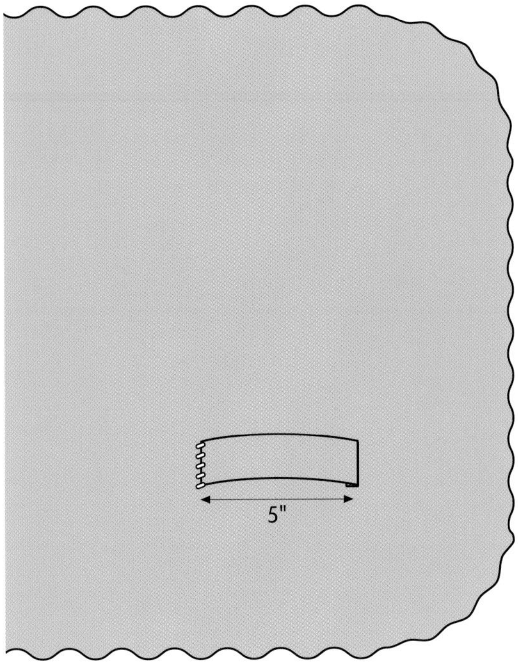

Making the Bow

1. Ruffle both long edges of the 4½" x 13" strip.

2. With the wrong side of the strip facing up, fold the short ends to the middle to make a loop, and hand stitch them together.

3. Fold the long edges of the 2" x 4" rectangle to the middle and wrap the folded strip around the bow center. Hand stitch the ends together, pulling the bow center tightly. Hand stitch the bow to the center of the shawl tab.

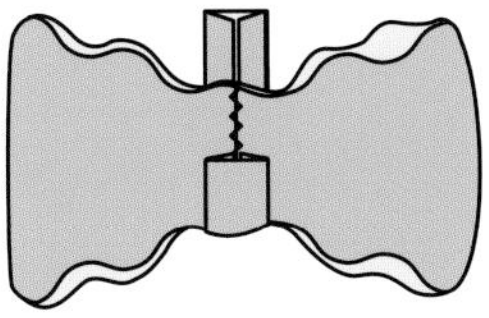

Just a Thought . . .

- If you prefer a longer shawl, add a center back seam and adjust the yardage accordingly to cut a second panel. The shawl length must be on the crosswise grain to ruffle properly.
- Not a fan of ruffles? Bind the edges for a more tailored look, or cut the fleece with a decorative rotary-cutter blade or scissors for a quick finish.
- On print fleece, consider adding some decorative stitching to accent the print. On solid fleece, use twin-needle stitching to create overall texture.

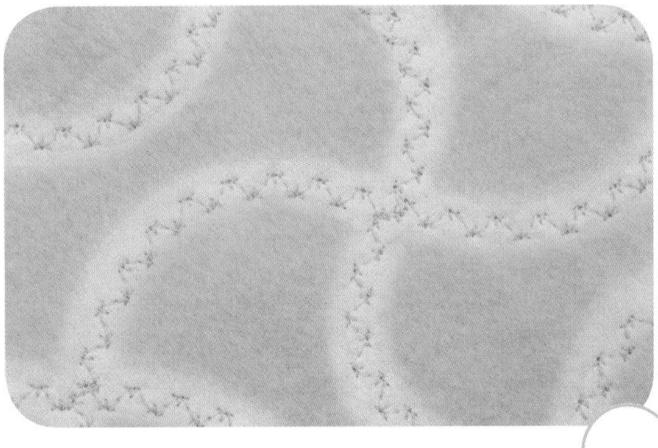

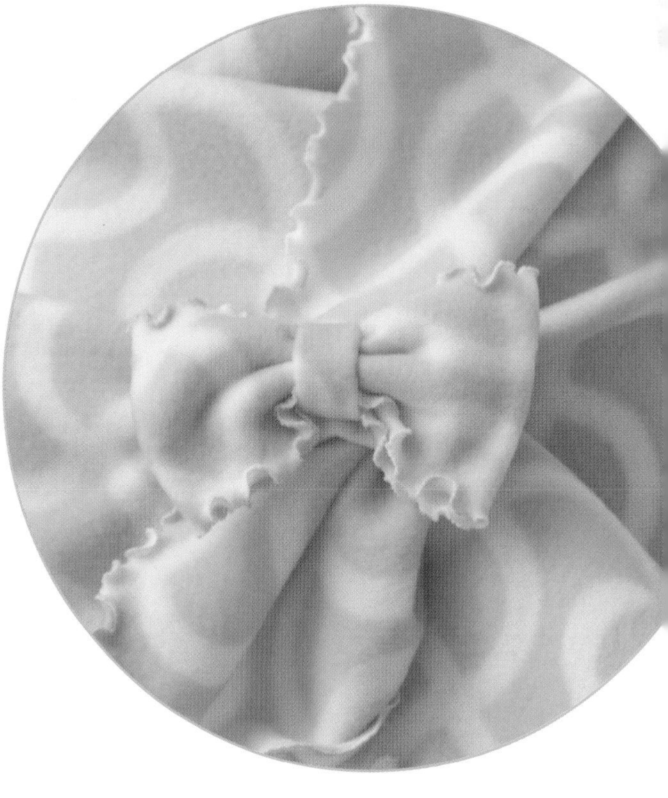

Punched-Up Poncho

by Linda Turner Griepentrog
Size: One size fits all

Who doesn't like a warm wrap? This snuggly poncho features a twin-needle ribbed collar that hugs your neck to keep the chill at bay. The one-size-fits-all nature makes it an ideal gift as well.

Make one for every season using your favorite fleece prints!

Materials

Yardage is based on 60"-wide fabric. Use a nondirectional print for the best results.

2 yards of fleece

4 mm or 6 mm twin needle

Chalk marker

Pattern-tracing material

Curved ruler (optional)

Needle Note

Some sewing machines can't accommodate a twin needle wider than 4 mm, so check your owner's manual for details. Other machines can use a 6 mm or 8 mm twin needle if you prefer larger pin tucks.

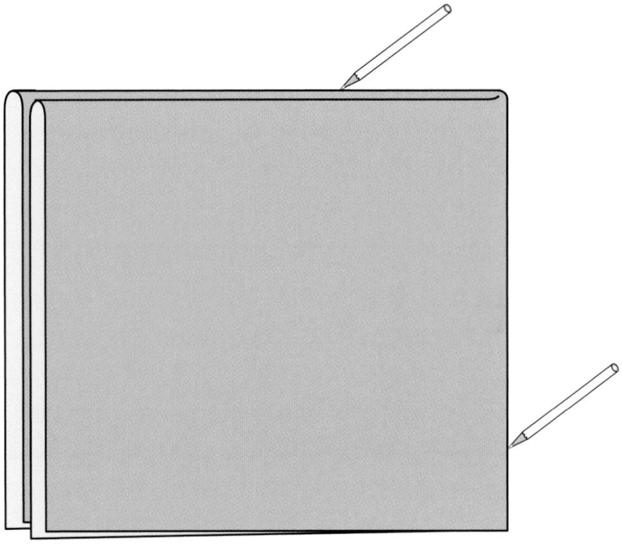

Cutting

Remove the selvages from the fabric before cutting. Trace the neckline pattern on pattern sheet 2 onto pattern-tracing material and cut it out.

From the fleece, cut:

1 rectangle, 54" x 60", with the lengthwise grain running parallel to the 60" measurement

1 strip, 8" x 34", with the lengthwise grain running parallel to the 8" measurement

Creating the Shape

1. Fold the fleece 54" x 60" rectangle in half vertically and horizontally and chalk-mark the folds to indicate the center front/back and shoulder lines as shown at right.

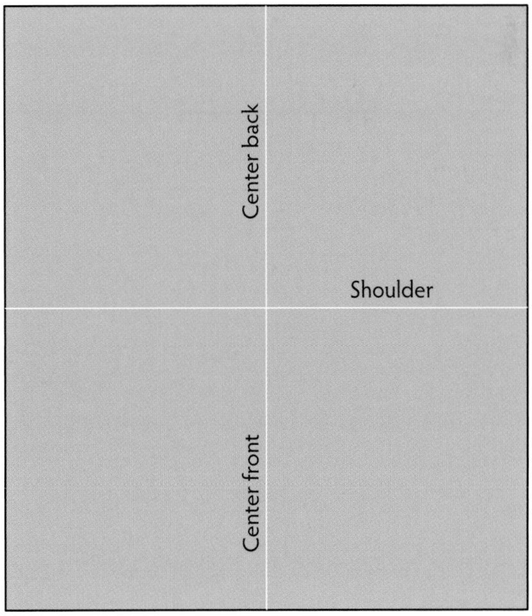

2. Unfold the rectangle. Pin the neckline pattern onto the rectangle, aligning the shoulder and center lines on the pattern with the chalk marks on the rectangle. Cut out the opening. Pin the neck edges together to avoid stretching them before the collar is inserted.

3. Using the curved ruler or a luncheon plate, round the corners of the fleece rectangle.

Making the Collar

1. Insert the twin needle into the machine. Set the stitch length to 3.5 mm and test the stitch on a fleece scrap, adjusting the tension as needed to create a raised pin tuck. Most machines require tightening the upper tension to make a raised tuck. Consult your owner's manual for specific setting requirements when using a twin needle.

2. When you're satisfied with the appearance of the tuck, stitch a row of pin tucking along the length of the 8" x 34" strip, beginning ¾" from one long edge. Using the edge of the presser foot as a guide, stitch multiple rows of pin tucks across the width of the strip, leaving at least ¼" unstitched on the side opposite the first row of pin tucking.

3. Because repeated stitching can distort the fabric size and shape, remeasure and trim the pin-tucked strip to the original dimensions, if needed.

4. Trim the collar strip ¼" beyond the final outermost tuck. Do not trim the first stitched side.

Finishing the Poncho Edges

1. Using the twin needle, stitch around the poncho perimeter 1¼" from the edge. Stitch a second row ¼" inside the first row.

2. Fold under the poncho outer edges along the first row of stitching. The fleece will naturally fold along the line of pin tucking. Change to a single needle and regular tension setting. Using a 3.5 mm stitch length, sew ¼" inside the second row of pin tucking, catching the hem on the wrong side.

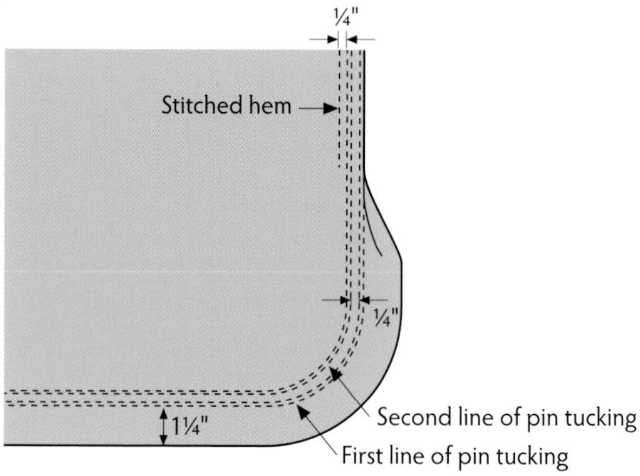

3. On the poncho wrong side, trim the hem edge close to the single stitching line.

Just a Thought . . .

Instead of pin tucking the finished edge, consider using a decorative rotary-cutter blade to cut out the rectangle, or bind the edges with a contrasting fabric.

Inserting the Collar

1. Clip the center front point of the neckline opening ⅜".

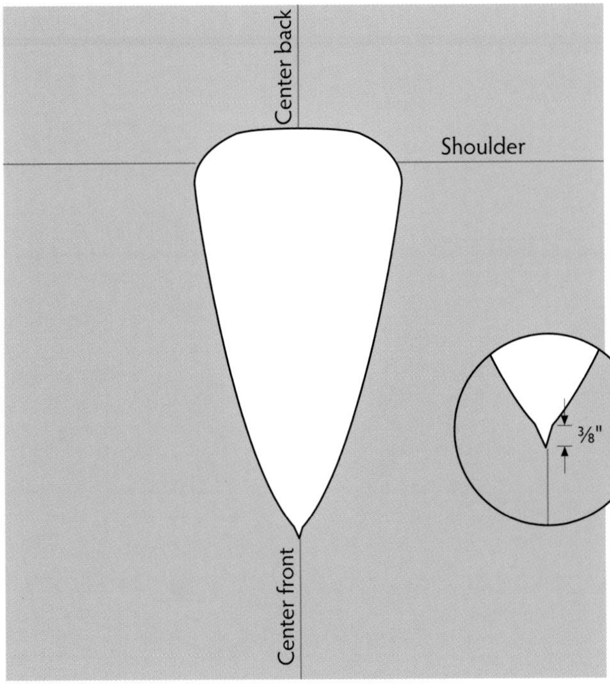

2. With the ¾"-wide unstitched edge toward the neckline edge, use a ½"-wide seam allowance to sew the short end of the collar to the neckline as shown. Pivot at the center-front point and continue stitching around the collar.

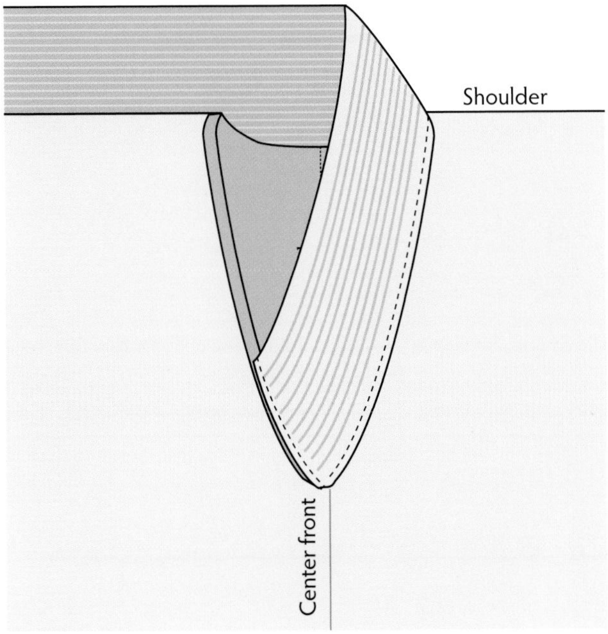

3. As you reach the starting point, place the remaining short end over the first end. If the collar is too long, trim the excess length. Sew the end of the collar in place over the first line of stitching.

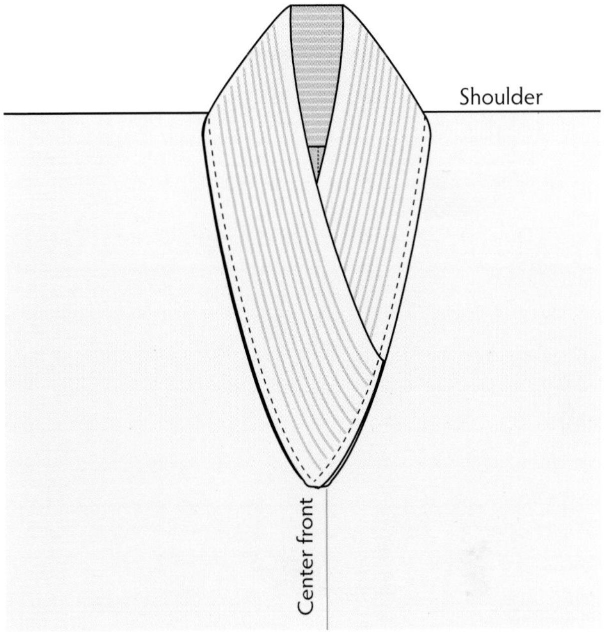

4. Finger-press the seam allowances toward the poncho, and then flatten and secure them by topstitching ¼" from the seamline.

Rapid Wrap

by Beth Bradley
Size: One size fits all

Create a super-simple draped wrap that makes an ideal layering piece for chilly days and fits just about everyone. The wrap is constructed from one large rectangle—no pattern needed!—and is easily customizable in width and length.

Curl up on the couch with this snuggly wrap!

Materials

Yardage is based on 60"-wide fabric.

1⅝ yards of fleece

Chalk marker

Curved ruler (optional)

Cutting

Remove the selvages from the fabric before cutting.

From the fleece, cut:

1 rectangle, 50" x 60" (if you're using a plaid, center the vertical repeat before cutting)

Preparing the Fabric

1. With the stretch running crosswise, fold the rectangle in half right sides together, carefully aligning all of the edges. Place the folded rectangle on a large, flat work surface.

2. On the top layer of fabric, mark the center points along the top folded edge and lower raw edge with the chalk marker. Draw a vertical line connecting the marks. Draw additional vertical lines 2½" from both sides of the center line to mark the center-front opening.

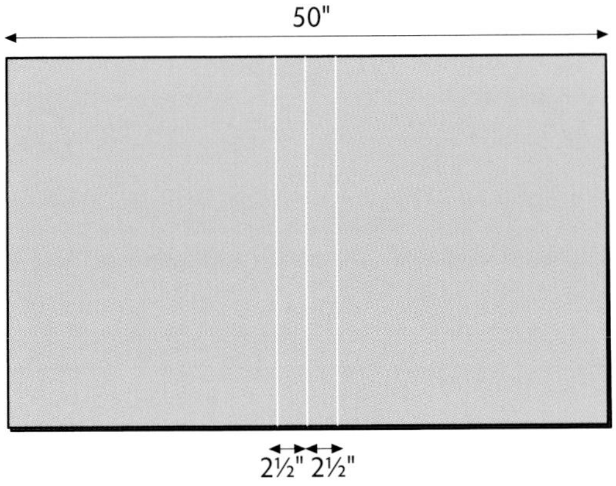

3. Cut along the center-front opening lines through the upper fabric layer only, and then cut carefully along the top folded edge between the two lines.

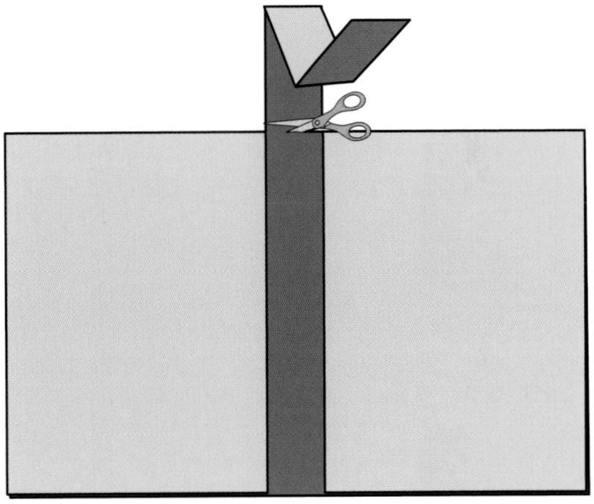

4. Mark the center of the top cut edge, and then measure 1" down and mark the center back point of the neckline. Using the curved ruler or another curved object such as a dinner plate, draw the back neckline curve by connecting the top folded edges through the center back point. Cut along the marked line.

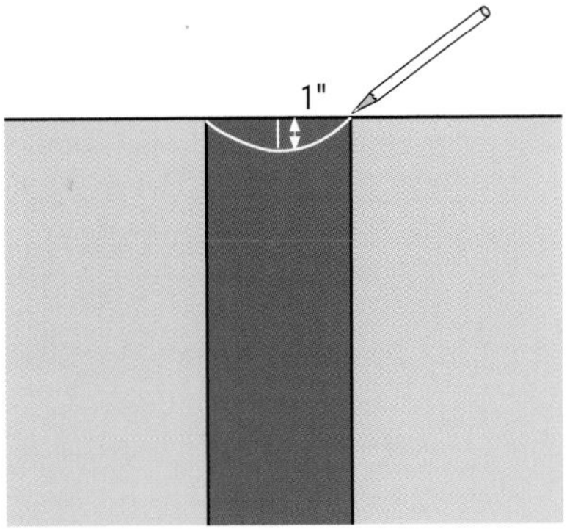

5. Turn the rectangle to the right side. Try on the wrap to determine whether you like the sleeve and body lengths. To shorten the sleeve or lower edges, pin-mark the desired finished lengths while the wrap is on your body. Remove the wrap, and then draw new cutting lines ½" beyond the pin marks to account for seam allowances. Make sure you remove the same amount from both sides to keep the sleeve length symmetrical.

Making the Wrap

1. Fold under the raw edges of the entire wrap, except for the back neckline, ½" to the wrong side; pin in place. To create crisp corners, fold under and pin the lower edges before folding under the side edges. Weave a pin through the layers at each corner for extra security.

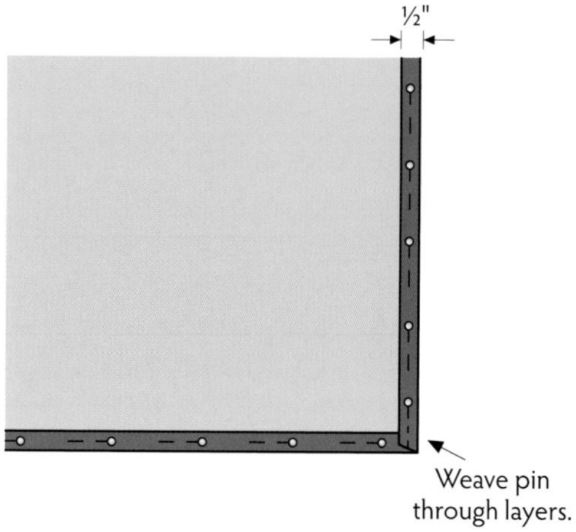

2. To create a smooth curve along the back neckline, fold under ¼" at the shoulder line, gradually increasing the folded amount to ½" at the center back point.

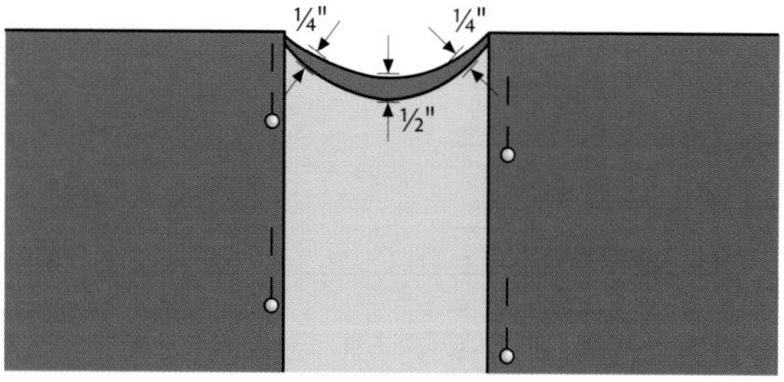

3. Using a 3.5 mm stitch length, sew all of the folded edges ⅛" from the hem raw edges. To avoid creating wavy edges, hold the fabric gently and don't stretch it as it goes through the machine. At each corner, stop with the needle down, and then pivot the fabric 90° to sew the adjacent edge. The multiple seam-allowance layers at the corners are bulky, so use a pin point or stiletto to guide the corner smoothly under the presser foot if needed.

4. Try on the wrap again, letting the front-opening corners fall open naturally. On one side of your body, hold out your arm so the front and back layers fall smoothly and evenly. Near your natural waistline, place a safety pin through both layers at whatever location is most flattering and comfortable. Lower your arms to determine if you are happy with the pin placement, and then pin again if needed.

5. With the safety pin still in place, remove the wrap and place it flat and right side up on the work surface. Make sure all of the layers and edges are evenly aligned and adjust the pinning if needed. At the safety-pin location, draw a 1"-long vertical mark. Repeat to draw a 1"-long mark at the identical location on the opposite side of the wrap. Place a pin horizontally at the top and bottom of each mark through both layers.

6. Stitch along each mark to anchor the front and back together, backstitching at the beginning and end. This tacking stitch provides shaping to the wrap when worn while allowing the sides to drape.

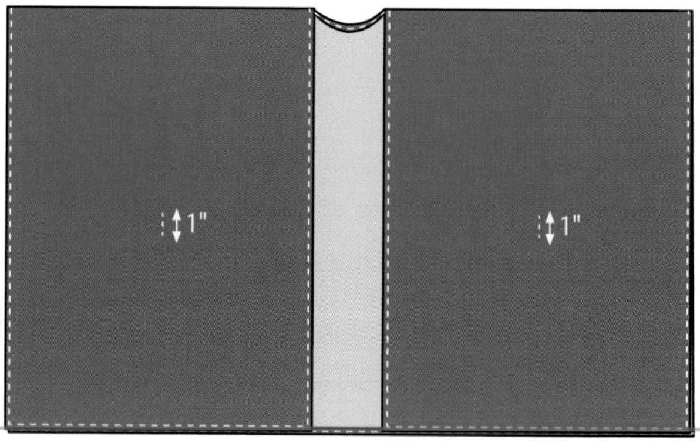

Sun, Moon, and Stars Pillow Trio

by Missy Shepler

Size: Each approximately 14" tall, not including the sun's rays

Create a cozy nest and nap the night—and day—away! These fun fleece pillows feature appliqués or textured "quilting" lines on the front. The star has an optional back pocket for stashing pajamas or nighttime reads.

Make a galaxy of stars to ensure sweet dreams.

Materials (for 3 pillows)

Yardage is based on 60"-wide fabric. Materials and cutting instructions for all 3 pillows are combined for the best use of yardage.

½ yard *each* of light-yellow, bright-yellow, and gold fleece

⅜ yard *each* of orange and cream fleece

Yellow or gold #5 pearl cotton

Polyester fiberfill

½ yard of lightweight sew-in nonwoven stabilizer (optional)

Pattern-tracing material

Large chenille hand-sewing needle

Cutting

Remove the selvages from the fabrics before cutting. Trace the moon and star pillow patterns on pattern sheet 1 onto pattern-tracing material, along with the patterns for the sun rays, moon dots, and hanging star. For the sun, see "Making the Sun Patterns" on page 45 for preparing the circle patterns.

From the light-yellow fleece, cut:
- 1 small star pillow front/back
- 1 medium sun pillow front/back
- 1 large sun pillow front/back
- 32 medium rays

From the bright-yellow fleece, cut:
- 1 strip, 1½" x 15"
- 1 small sun pillow front/back
- 1 medium star pillow front/back
- 2 small hanging stars

From the gold fleece, cut:
- 2 large star pillow front/backs
- 1 large sun pillow front/back
- 32 large rays
- 2 large spots
- 2 small spots
- 2 medium hanging stars

From the orange fleece, cut:
- 1 strip, 4" x 53"
- 1 large star pillow pocket
- 32 triangle rays
- 1 large hanging star

From the cream fleece, cut:
- 1 moon pillow front/back
- 1 reversed moon pillow front/back

Just a Thought . . .

To make quick work of cutting the sun rays, cut strips, and then subcut the triangular pieces from the strips, using the sun ray patterns as a guide. Cut 3¾"-wide strips for the gold large rays and 3"-wide strips for the light-yellow medium rays and orange triangle rays.

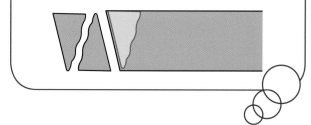

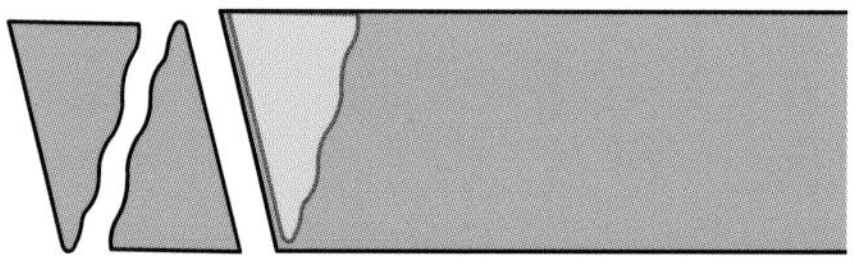

Moon Pillow

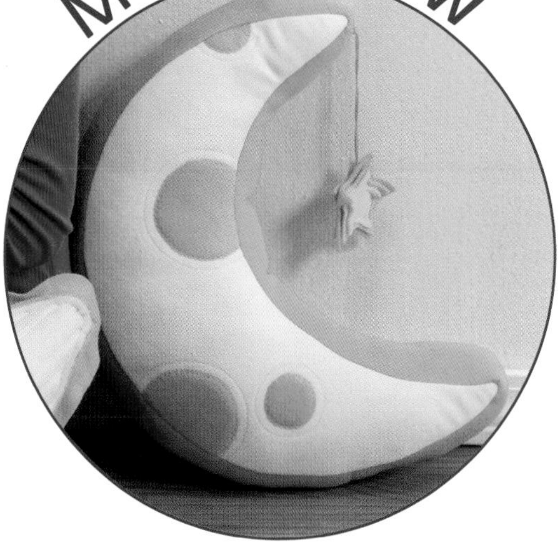

Assembling the Pillow

For a sturdier pillow, apply lightweight sew-in stabilizer to the wrong side of the front and back pieces.

1. Referring to the moon front/back pattern for placement, position the large and small spots right side up on the right side of the pillow front. Pin or use temporary spray adhesive to secure the spots in place.

2. Carefully stitch around the outer edge of each spot using a straight, zigzag, or decorative stitch. Topstitch around each spot, ¼" from the outer edges. Trim the spots even with the outer edges of the pillow front.

3. Fold under one end of the orange 4" x 53" strip 1" to the wrong side and pin it in place. With right sides together and starting with the folded end, pin one long edge of the strip to the outer edge of the pillow front, taking care not to stretch either edge. Fold under the remaining short end to the wrong side so that the short strip ends abut.

4. Sew the strip to the pillow front. To reinforce the seam, stitch again, ¼" from the first line of stitching.

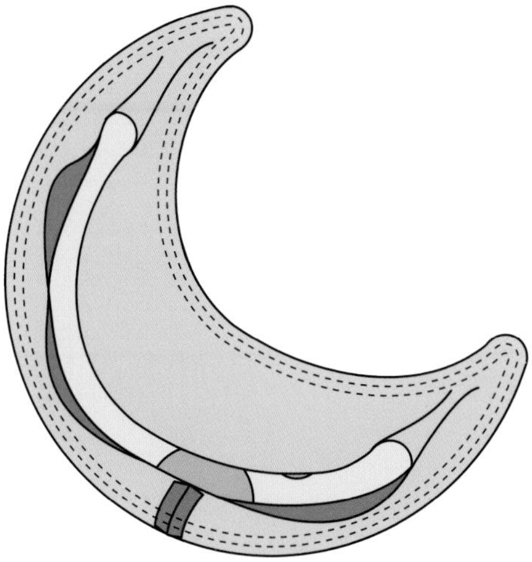

5. Pin the unsewn strip edge to the right side of the pillow back, making sure the back is oriented to mirror the front. Sew the strip to the pillow back. To reinforce the seam, stitch again, ¼" from the first line of stitching.

6. Turn the pillow right side out through the strip opening where the ends met and finger-press the seam allowances toward the strip.

7. Gently stuff the pillow with polyester fiberfill, making sure to fill both curved points and being careful not to stretch the fleece. Slip-stitch the opening closed.

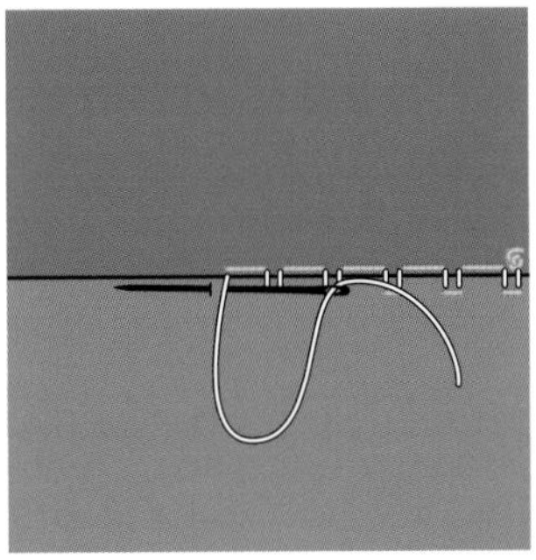

Making the Hanging Star

1. Cut three 12" lengths of pearl cotton and tie them together with an overhand knot close to one end. Place the knotted end against the wrong side of the orange large hanging star, with the knotted end 1" below the top point of the star. Sew the pearl cotton to the hanging star, stitching just above the knot.

2. Stack the small, medium, and large hanging-star layers as shown, aligning the points and centering the stars. The top three stars will face right side up. The bottom two stars will face wrong side up. The sewn end of the pearl cotton will be sandwiched between the stacked stars. Pin the layers in place.

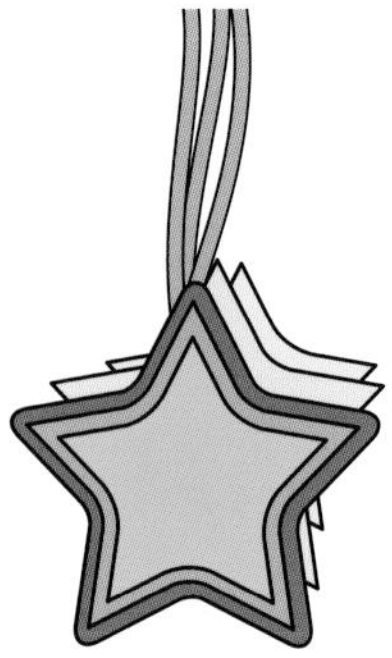

3. Sew very carefully ¼" inside the outer edge of the center star to secure the layers.

4. Using a large chenille hand-sewing needle, secure the loose ends of the pearl cotton to the upper tip of the moon pillow, adjusting the star to hang about 4" below the tip of the moon.

Star Pillow

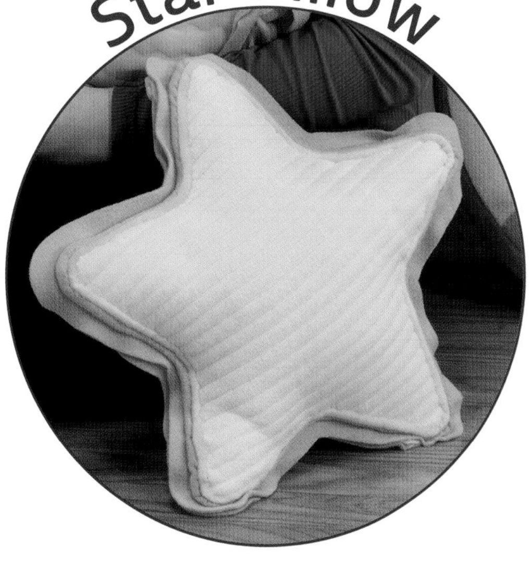

Assembling the Pillow Front

1. With right sides up, center the small light-yellow star over the medium bright-yellow star, and then center the layered star unit over the large gold star. Generously pin the layers together, placing the pins horizontally.

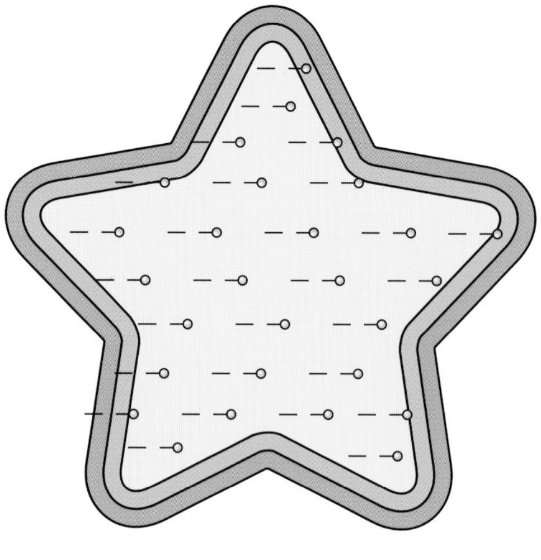

2. Topstitch straight vertical lines ½" to 1" apart through the layered stars, starting and stopping at the edges of the small star and removing pins just before you come to them.

3. Roll the unstitched edge of the medium star toward the center of the pillow, forming a rolled edge. Slip-stitch the inner edge of the roll to the small star.

Assembling the Pillow Back

1. With right sides together, align one long edge of the bright-yellow 1½" x 15" strip with the long straight edge of the orange pocket piece. Sew the strip to the pocket using a scant ½"-wide seam allowance.

2. Fold the strip up and over the long straight edge of the pocket. Pin the strip in place, covering the seam allowance. From the right side, topstitch just below the folded strip, catching the unsewn strip edge on the back of the pocket. Trim the strip even with the star edges.

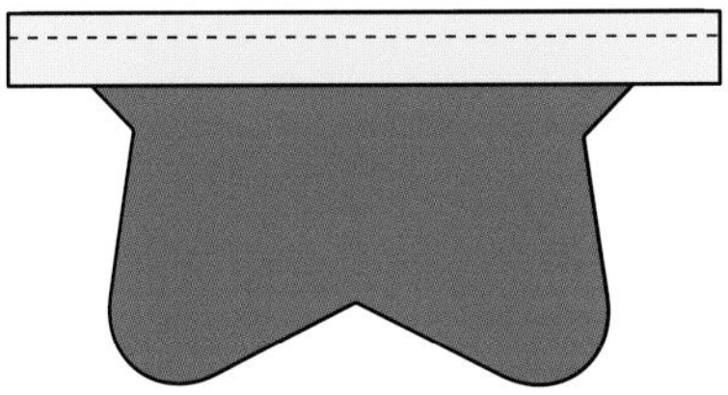

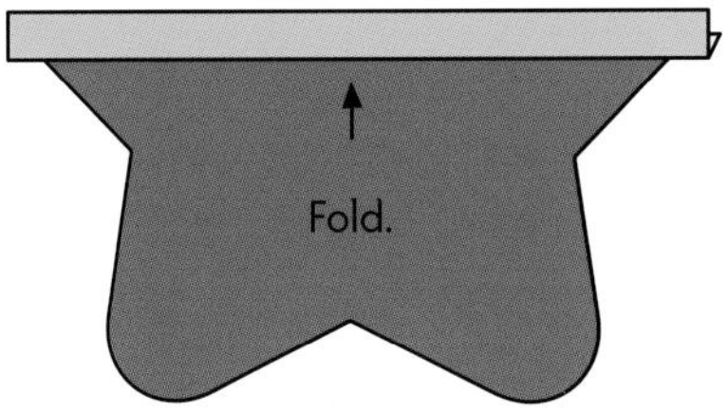

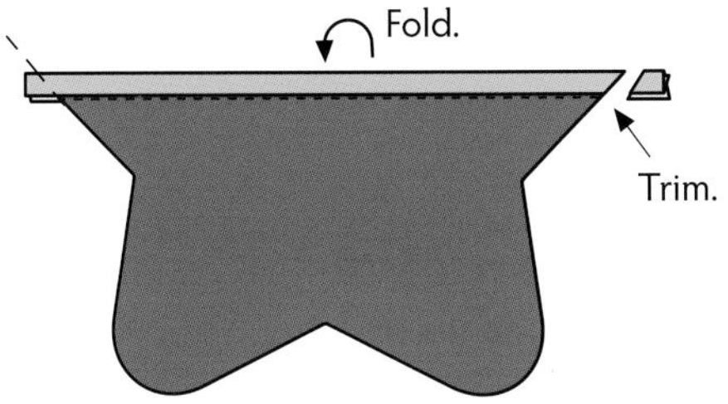

3. Place the wrong side of the pocket against the right side of the remaining large star, matching the outer edges. Pin in place.

Completing the Pillow

1. Place the pillow front and back wrong sides together, matching the outer edges. Pin, and then sew the large stars together close to the rolled edge of the medium star. Leave a 4" opening for stuffing.

2. On the pillow front, roll the outer edge of the large star toward the center of the pillow so it forms a rolled edge next to the previous rolled edge. Use a slip stitch to secure the rolled edge in place.

3. Gently stuff the pillow with polyester fiberfill, making sure to fill all five star points and being careful not to stretch the fleece. Slipstitch the opening closed.

Sun Pillow

Making the Sun Patterns

1. Use a pencil or marking pen and a length of string to make a compass. You'll need to draw a 13"-, 14"-, and 15"-diameter circle onto a large sheet of paper. First, tie the string around the pencil, measure 7½" from the pencil, and use a thumbtack to hold the string in place in the center of the paper. Using the pencil as a compass, hold the thumbtack with one hand, and with the string held taut, draw a circle with the pencil as shown.

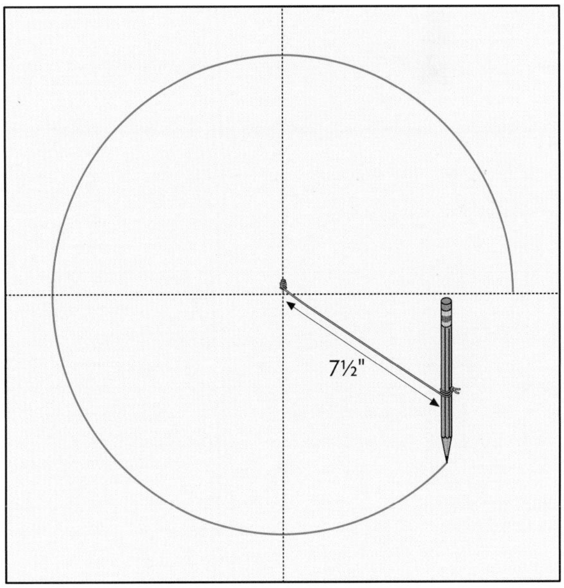

2. Repeat to make a 14" circle and a 13" circle pattern, adjusting the string length so it is half the length of the desired circle diameter.

3. See "Cutting" on page 42 for which fabrics to use for each circle.

Assembling the Pillow Front

1. With right sides up, center the small bright-yellow, medium light-yellow, and large gold sun front/back circles on top of each other as shown. Generously pin the layers together, placing the pins vertically.

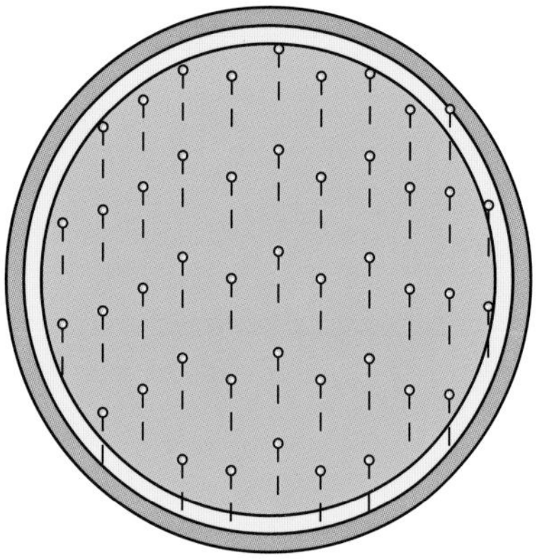

2. Topstitch serpentine horizontal lines ½" to 1" apart through the layered circles, starting and stopping at the outer edges of the small circle.

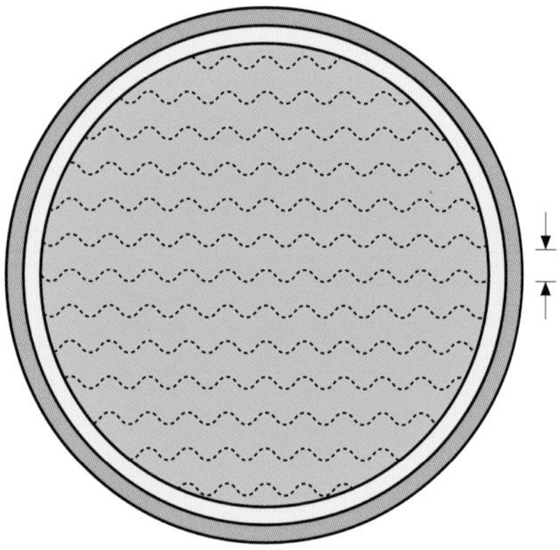

Assembling the Pillow Back

1. Center one light-yellow medium ray right side up on top of the right side of one gold large ray, aligning the flat bottom edges. Zigzag around the two long edges of the medium ray to appliqué it to the large ray. Repeat with the remaining ray pieces.

2. Place the light-yellow large sun front/back circle wrong side up on a flat surface. Arrange the appliquéd rays from step 1 and the orange triangle rays right side up in layers around the outer edge of the pillow back, making sure to overlap the outer edge of the pillow back 1½". Pin the rays in place, and then stitch ¼" from the base of the rays to secure them.

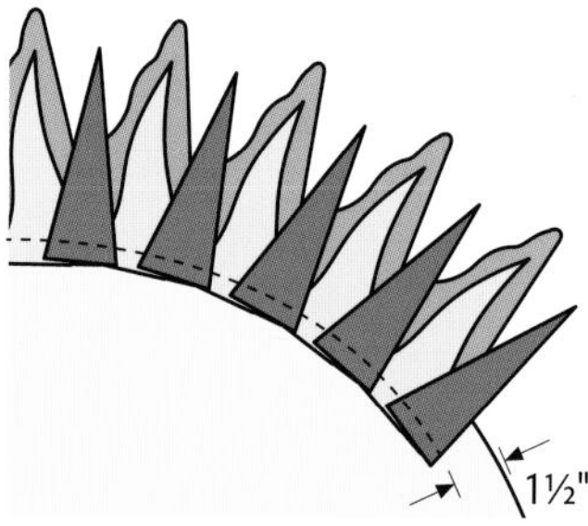

Completing the Pillow

1. Place the pillow front and back wrong sides together, matching the outer edges of the large circles. Pin, and then sew the pillow front and back together, sewing just outside the small bright-yellow circle and leaving a 4" opening for stuffing. Take care not to catch the loose ends of the rays in the seam.

2. Gently stuff the pillow with polyester fiberfill, making sure not to stretch the fleece, and sew the opening closed.

Pillow-Power Loungers

by Linda Turner Griepentrog
Sizes: 27" x 80" (4-pillow); 27" x 60" (3-pillow)

Perfect for sleepovers or watching TV, these roll-up loungers get their support from simple standard-size bed pillows. When they're not in use, stow the pillows and fold up the fleece cases for easy storage.

Make a great napping spot for kids!

Materials

Yardage is based on 60"-wide fabric.

For the 4-pillow version

2⅜ yards of print fleece

1⅓ yards of ¾"-wide Velcro

4 standard-size bed pillows

For the 3-pillow version

1¾ yards of print fleece

5⅛ yards of ⅝"-wide grosgrain ribbon

3 standard-size bed pillows

Cutting

Remove the selvages from the fabric before cutting. If there isn't a full 60" remaining, the fabric can still be used; just replace the new width measurement for the 60" measurement in the cutting dimensions.

For the 4-pillow version

From the print fleece, cut:
1 rectangle, 60" x 81"

For the 3-pillow version

From the print fleece, cut:
1 rectangle, 60" x 61"

Making the Lounger

1. With right sides together, fold the rectangle across the fabric width. Stitch each end using a ½"-wide seam allowance. Sew the seam with a narrow zigzag stitch (2.0 mm width, 2.0 mm length) to maintain the fabric's stretch.

2. Turn the rectangle right side out and lay it on a flat surface. Turn under the long cut edges 1½" and pin or clip the hem in place. Stitch 1¼" from the turned-under edge.

3. With the lounger lying flat and the stitched seam at either end, chalk-mark either three or four 20" sections, depending on which size you're making. Stitch the sections in place across the folded fabric width to make the pillow compartments.

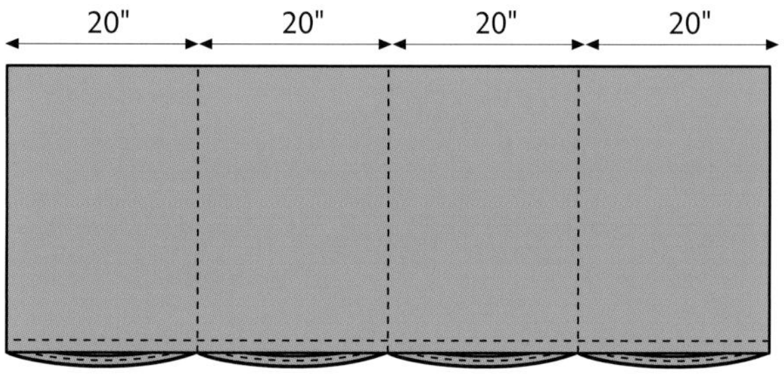

Completing the 4-Pillow Lounger

1. Cut the Velcro into four lengths, 12" each.

2. Center the hook side of the Velcro on the same side of the lounger hem on each pillow section, approximately ¼" from the hem edge. Stitch around each Velcro section.

3. Repeat step 2 to attach the loop section of the Velcro to the opposite half of each hemmed section in the corresponding location.

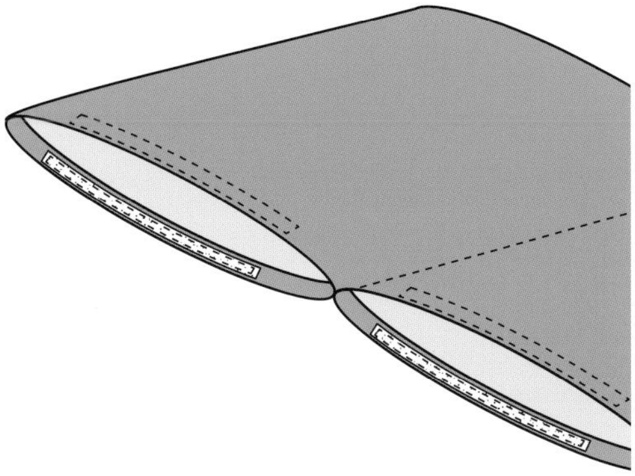

Completing the 3-Pillow Lounger

1. Cut the ribbon into 12 lengths, 15" each.

2. Pin one ribbon length into each pillow section 6" from the sewn seam, extending the length just past the hem stitching line. Stitch a box at the end of each ribbon to attach it to the pillow hem. Repeat for the opposite half of each pillow opening.

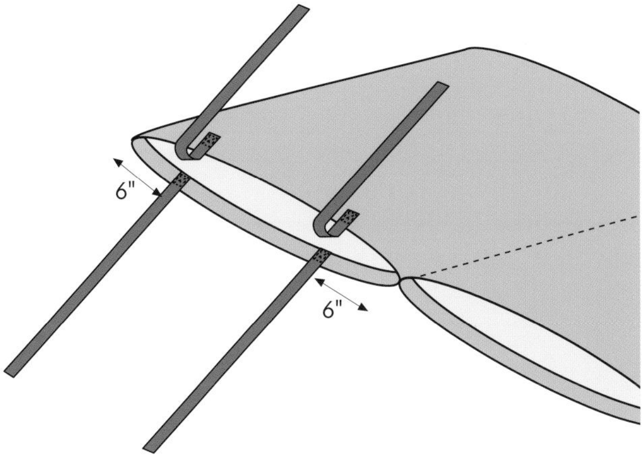

3. Trim the ribbon ends at an angle if desired.

Using the Lounger

1. Insert a firm, standard-size bed pillow into each section of the lounger and secure the opening edges by either pressing the two segments of Velcro together or tying the ribbons into bows.

2. Position the lounger flat on the floor for lying down, or fold back one of the pillow sections to prop up the user's head in a reclining position.

Just a Thought . . .

Make this lounger longer and use it for an adult—not only for TV watching, reading, and an occasional overnight guest, but perhaps in outdoor fabric for use on the patio chaise.

Hex Mix Blanket

Die-cutter friendly!

by Missy Shepler

Finished size: Approximately 58" x 70"

Create a honeycomb of hexagons held in place by simple straight stitching on this quick-to-make blanket. A single-layer binding adds the finishing touch.

Sew a seamless blanket that's big on style and a cinch to make.

Materials

Yardage is based on 60"-wide fabric.

2 yards of cream fleece for background

1 yard *total* of assorted print and solid fleeces for hexagons

½ yard of fleece for binding

Cutting

Remove the selvages from the fabrics before cutting. The hexagon pattern is on pattern sheet 2.

From the assorted print and solid fleeces, cut a *total* of:

60 hexagons

1 rectangle, 1" x 2½"

From the binding fleece, cut:

5 strips, 2¼" x 60"

Assembling the Blanket

1. Trim the selvages from the cream fleece and square up the cut edges. Fold the piece wrong sides together, matching the cut edges and creating a rectangle approximately 58" x 35". Chalk- or pin-mark the folded edge to mark the horizontal center. Unfold and refold the fleece in the opposite direction to mark the vertical center along the folded edge.

2. Unfold the fleece and lay it right side up on a flat surface, being careful not to stretch the fleece.

3. Place one hexagon right side up just to the left of the marked center, aligning the side points of the hexagon with the horizontal center line. Using the 1" x 2½" rectangle as a spacing guide, place two hexagons directly above and two hexagons directly below the first hexagon. Pin the vertical row of hexagons in place as shown at right.

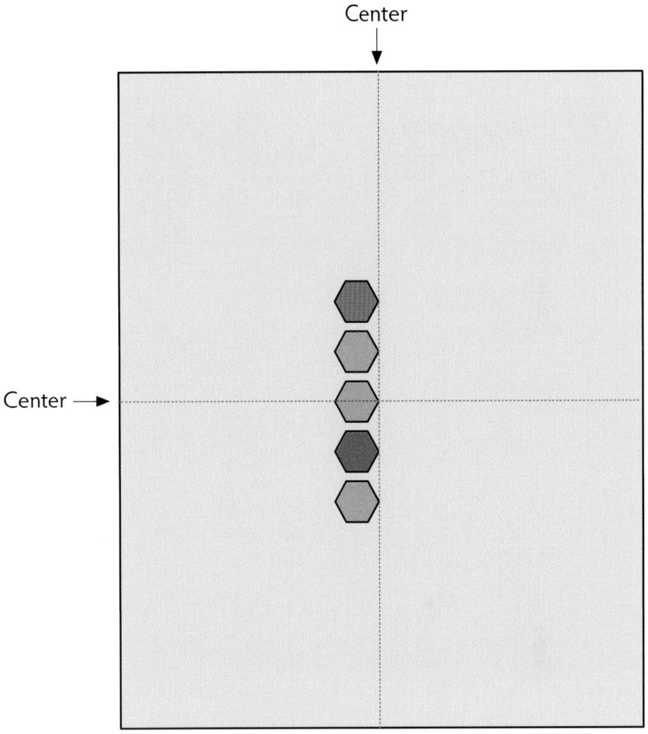

4. Place the remaining hexagons in vertical rows parallel to the first row, offsetting every other row as shown. Randomly select one hexagon to move to the open area at the top of the blanket; move a second hexagon to the open area at the bottom of the blanket. Pin the hexagons in place.

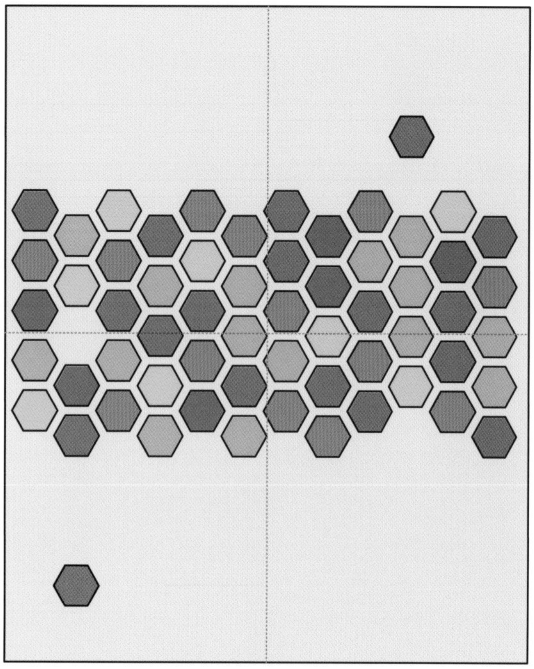

5. Sew multiple straight lines ½" apart from one side of the blanket to the other across the grouped area of hexagons to secure them. Secure the two hexagons in the open areas with straight lines of topstitching ½" apart, starting and stopping at the edges of the hexagons.

Just a Thought . . .

Add a little extra interest by using several thread colors to topstitch the hexagons to the background.

Finishing the Blanket

1. Sew the 2¼" x 60" binding strips together end to end to make one long strip, using a diagonal seam to help distribute the bulk. Trim the seam allowances to ⅛".

2. With right sides together, sew one long edge of the binding strip to the outer edge of the blanket using a scant ½"-wide seam allowance and mitering the corners. Fold the raw edge of the binding strip to the wrong side, enclosing the outer edge of the blanket. Pin the folded binding in place. Working from the right side of the blanket, topstitch just below the inner edge of the binding, catching the binding on the back of the blanket.

3. Carefully trim the excess binding from the back of the blanket, cutting close to the stitching.

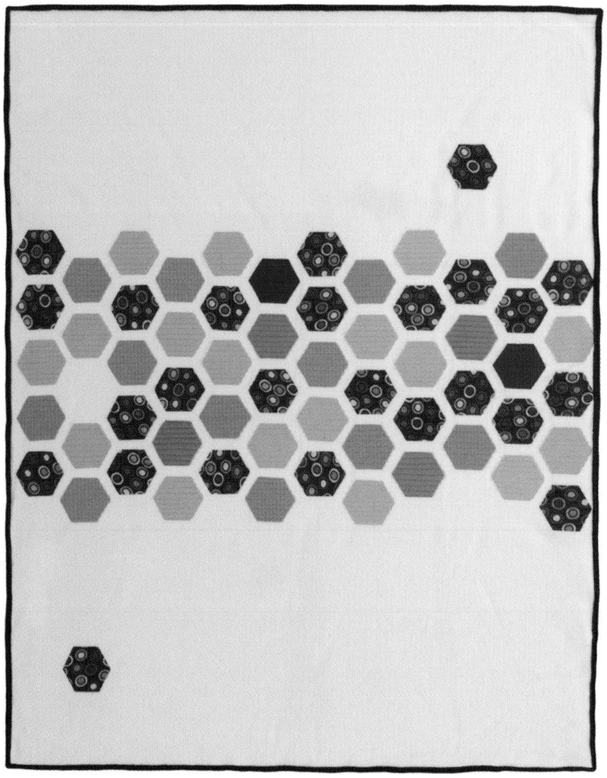

Hank the Hound

by Missy Shepler
Size: Approximately 14" x10"

Our fleece friend Hank is all hound, and he has the oversize schnoz to prove it! This cuddly canine sports contrasting spots, plus exposed seams for easier sewing.

Prepare to make a litter of these pups! Everyone will want one.

Materials

Yardage is based on 60"-wide fabric.

½ yard of cream fleece for body

18" x 18" square of teal fleece for contrasting accents

¾ yard of lightweight sew-in nonwoven stabilizer

Polyester fiberfill

2 teal round beads, ⅜" diameter

1 white button, ⅜" diameter

Pattern-tracing material

Cutting

Remove the selvages from the cream fleece before cutting. Trace the patterns on pattern sheet 2 onto pattern-tracing material and cut them out. Use the patterns to cut the pieces below.

From the cream fleece, cut:

- 1 body
- 1 reversed body
- 1 belly
- 1 head gusset
- 1 ear
- 1 reversed ear
- 1 tail
- 1 reversed tail

From the teal fleece, cut:

- 1 strip, ⅝" x 12½"
- 1 ear
- 1 reversed ear
- 4 paws
- 1 nose

From the stabilizer, cut:

- 1 body
- 1 reversed body
- 1 belly
- 1 head gusset

Adding the Appliqués

1. If desired, make a one-of-a-kind hound by appliquéing unique spots to the body pieces. Plan your spots by referring to the photo on page 53 for placement, or by drawing corresponding shapes on the body pattern. Use the drawn shapes as a guide, or simply cut softly rounded shapes from the remaining teal fleece. In any places where spots will cross a seam, take care to extend the shapes into the seam allowances.

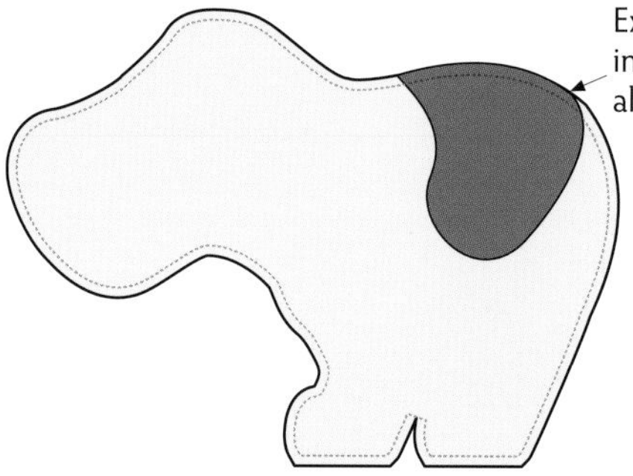
Extend spot
into seam
allowance.

2. Place the spots right side up on the right side of the body pieces and pin in place. Carefully stitch around the outer edge of each spot using a straight, zigzag, or decorative stitch of your choice. Sew slowly, taking care to secure the outer edges of each appliqué.

3. Referring to the pattern placement lines, position the nose right side up on the right side of the head gusset. Carefully stitch around the outer edge of the nose using a straight, zigzag, or decorative stitch of your choice.

Assembling the Hound

1. Pin or use temporary spray adhesive to secure the stabilizer to the wrong side of the corresponding body, belly, and head gusset pieces.

2. Pin-mark each end of the center line of the belly piece. With wrong sides together, align one half of the belly piece with the leg section of one body piece. Pin, then sew the belly to the body, leaving the paw bottoms unsewn and stopping at the pin-marked center points of the belly piece.

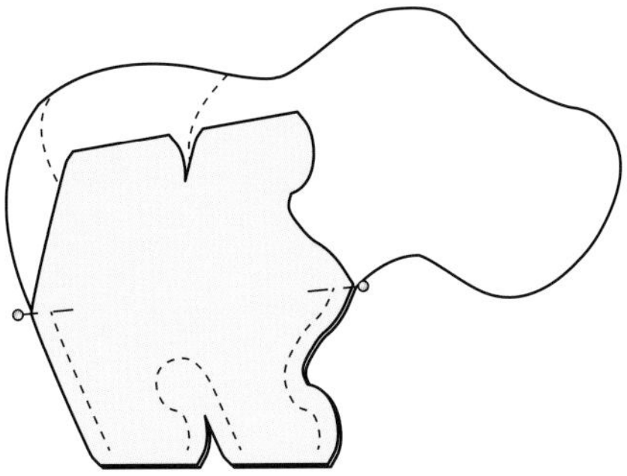

3. With wrong sides together, sew the opposite side of the belly piece to the remaining body piece, leaving the paw bottoms unsewn.

4. With wrong sides together, align one long edge of the head gusset to one body, matching points A and B. Pin, and then sew the gusset in place. Repeat to sew the opposite long edge of the head gusset to the remaining body piece.

5. Pin, and then sew the body pieces together between point B and the center-front belly seam.

6. Place the tail pieces wrong sides together, aligning the outer edges. Stitch ¼" from the outer edges, leaving the base of the tail unstitched. Lightly stuff the tail with polyester fiberfill. Pin the tail in place at the back of the dog, overlapping the body seam by ¼" and matching the C points.

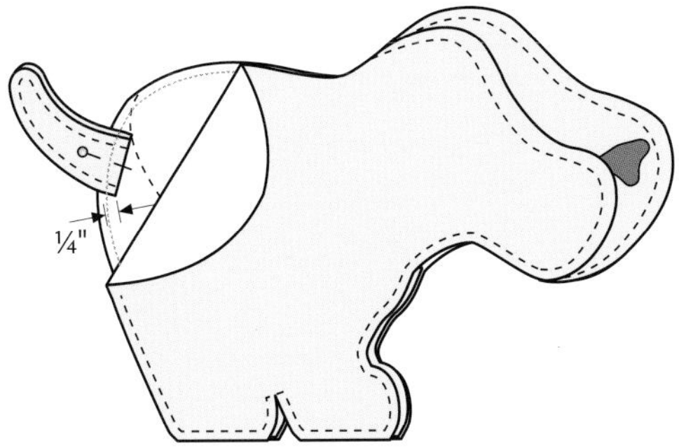

7. Pin, and then sew the body pieces together between point A and the center-back belly seam, catching the base of the tail in the seamline.

8. Carefully trim the stabilizer in the seam allowances close to the seamlines.

9. Gently stuff the hound, pushing the fiberfill into the body through the open bottoms of the paws. Fill the nose first, packing the stuffing enough to make a firm but soft toy. Try not to stretch the fleece.

10. Hand sew one paw piece to the base of each leg, folding the outer edges of the paw pieces to the wrong side as needed to cover the openings.

Finishing the Hound

1. Place one ear and one reversed ear wrong sides together. Using a ¼"-wide seam allowance, stitch around the outer edge of the ear. Repeat with the remaining pieces to make a second ear.

2. Referring to the photo for placement, fold the bottom edge of each ear in half and pin in place on the hound's head. Whipstitch around the sides and bottom edge of each ear, securing the ears to the head.

3. Referring to the head gusset pattern for placement, sew two beads or buttons to the head gusset for eyes.

4. Loop the teal ⅝" x 12½" strip around the hound's neck, overlapping the ends 1". Hand tack the overlapped ends together. Sew a button over the stitching to hide the tacked ends.

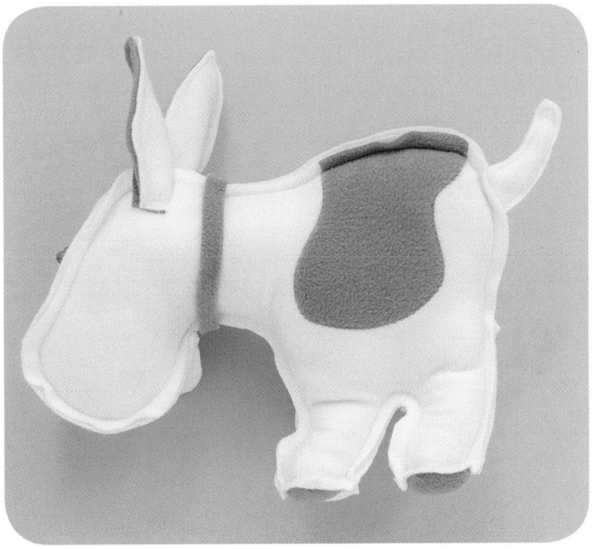

Comfy Pet Perch and Toy

by Linda Turner Griepentrog

Finished size: 22" x 36" x 2"

A personalized bed is the ultimate luxury for any of our best friends, and except for the lettering, there's not even a stitch needed to put this one together. Use your pet's name or simply a generic phrase like "WOOF."

Your pet will be so comfy he may not come when called.

Materials

Yardage is based on 60"-wide fabric.

2 yards of animal-themed fleece
8" x 16" rectangle of white fleece
22" x 36" x 2" foam slab
Chalk marker
Tear-away stabilizer
Temporary spray adhesive
Small, sharp-pointed embroidery scissors
Fringe-cutting tool (optional)

Cutting

Remove the selvages from the fabric before cutting.

From the animal-themed fleece, cut:
2 rectangles, 34" x 48"

Changing the Bed Size

To make the bed a different size, choose the foam first, and then determine the necessary fleece size as follows: The fleece should be the cut size of the foam, plus one-half the foam depth on *each* side, plus 10" total for fringe. For example, a kitty bed that's 15" x 20" x 2" would require two rectangles of cut fleece, each 27" x 32".

Preparing the Bed

1. Lay the two fleece rectangles wrong sides together on a flat surface, matching the cut edges. Chalk-mark a line 5" from each cut edge.

2. Cut a 5" square from each corner, cutting through both layers. Cut ½"- to ¾"-wide fringe on all sides of the doubled fleece rectangles, cutting from the raw edges up to the chalk-marked lines through both layers. It's important to cut both rectangles together so that you have the same number of fringe strands on each layer.

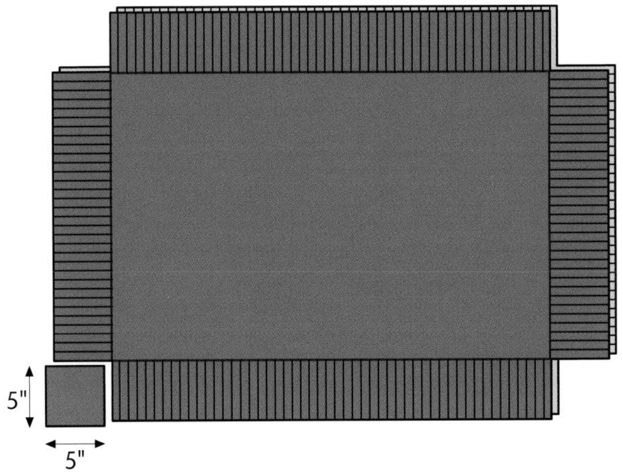

3. Lift off the top layer of slashed fleece and center it, right side up, over the foam slab. Chalk-mark a suitable location for the lettering.

Appliquéing the Letters

1. Trace the *W-O-O-F* letters on pattern sheet 2 onto tear-away stabilizer (see "Just a Thought..." on page 58 for other ideas).

2. Spray temporary adhesive on the wrong side of the white fleece rectangle and position it over the letter-location marking on the top fleece rectangle. Spray the underside of the tear-away stabilizer and position the lettering in the marked location over the white fleece.

3. Using a straight stitch or a tiny zigzag stitch, stitch around the lettering through all the layers. Remove the stabilizer. Using sharp-pointed embroidery scissors, carefully trim the white fleece layer *only* just outside the stitching lines.

Assembling the Bed

1. Lay the bottom fringed rectangle wrong side up on a flat surface. Center the foam slab over the bottom rectangle, and then center the top rectangle over the foam slab.

2. Beginning at one corner, tie together a fringe strand from the top fleece layer and the corresponding one from the bottom fleece layer. They can be joined in a square knot or an overhand knot, depending on your preference. Pull the strands tightly against the foam before tying.

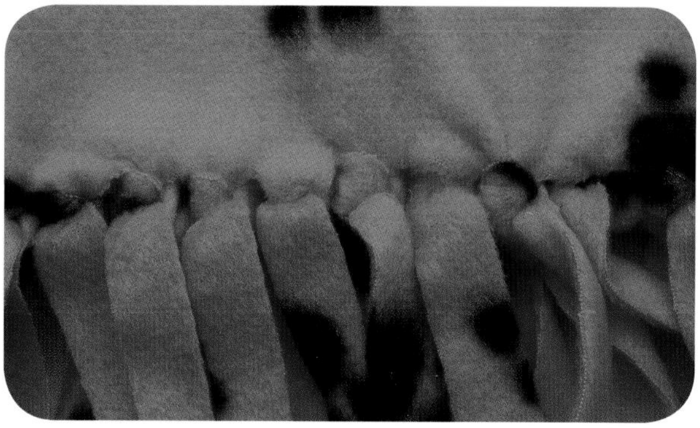

Use a square knot to join.

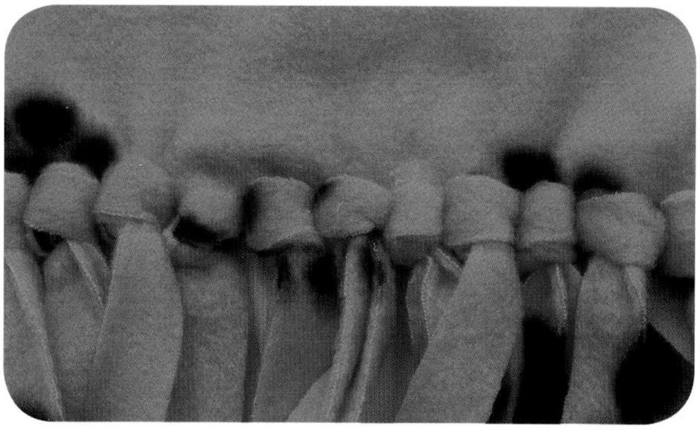

Try an overhand knot for a different look.

3. If your pet is prone to chewing things, trim the fringe ends about 1" from the knots; otherwise, simply leave the long fringe ends intact.

Just a Thought . . .

- To personalize the bed with your pet's name or other saying, use free online clip art for alphabet letters or draw your own. Words or names can be positioned on one or both ends of the bed, or down either or both sides.

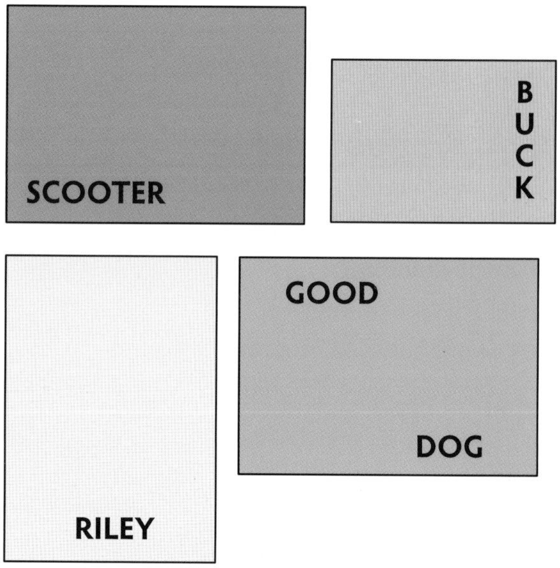

- Make each side of the bed from a different-color fabric for added fun.
- For an extra-plush touch, add a layer of thick batting over the top of the foam slab. Use temporary spray adhesive to hold it in place while covering it with the fleece.

Bonus Project!

Use the scraps from the bed to make a tug-of-war toy for your pooch. Cut three 2" x 24" strips of fleece, join them with an overhand knot at one end, and then tightly braid the lengths as far as you can. Tie an overhand knot at the remaining end to secure.

Kitty Tunnel and Toys

by Missy Shepler
Size: Approximately 14" tall

Keep feline friends entertained with an interactive tunnel toy. Tuck treats, toys, or catnip in the easy-to-add pocket strip. Emergency-blanket inserts add crinkle and reflect warmth, so this toy does double-duty as a cozy kitty clubhouse.

Create a tunnel that's the cat's meow for furry felines.

Materials

Yardage is based on 60"-wide fabric.

1 yard of print fleece

⅛ yard of coordinating solid fleece

1 yard of 1"-thick 27"-wide Poly-Fil Nu-Foam (a compressed, densified polyester batting)

1 emergency thermal blanket

2½ yards of 18-gauge craft wire (optional)

Large safety pin or bodkin

Cutting

Remove the selvages from the fabrics before cutting.

From the print fleece, cut:
- 1 rectangle, 35" x 41"
- 1 strip, 4½" x 35"
- 2 strips, 4" x 35"

From the coordinating solid fleece, cut:
- 1 strip, 4" x 35"

From the emergency thermal blanket, cut:
- 1 strip, 13" x width of blanket
- 1 strip, 10" x width of blanket

From the densified batting, cut:
- 1 strip, 13½" x 36"

Preparing the Tunnel Cover

Turn under one long edge of the 35" x 41" rectangle 1" to the wrong side. Topstitch ½" from the turned-under edge to make a hem.

Adding the Pocket Strip

1. Turn under one long edge of the 4½" x 35" pocket strip ½" to the wrong side. Topstitch ¼" from the turned-under edge to create a hemmed pocket edge.

2. Center the pocket strip right side up on the 35" x 41" rectangle, with the hemmed edge of the pocket strip 2½" from and parallel to the unhemmed edge of the rectangle. **Note:** The pocket strip does not extend all the way across the rectangle. Fold the long unhemmed edge and sides of the pocket strip ½" to the wrong side. Pin the pocket strip to the rectangle. Topstitch the sides and lower edge of the pocket strip in place, ¼" from the folded edges.

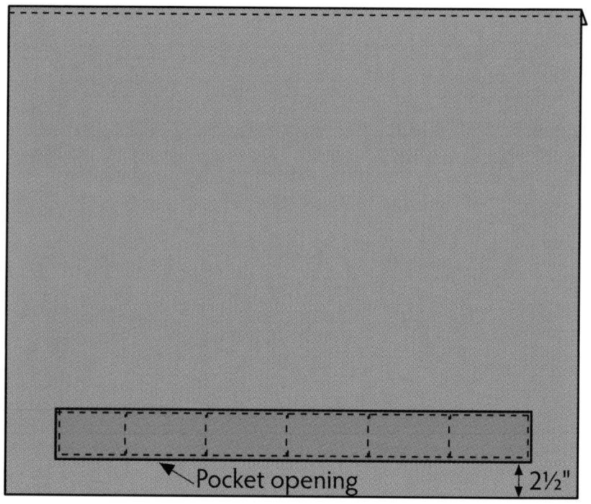

3. Divide the pocket strip into smaller individual pockets by sewing short seams perpendicular to the long strip edges, spacing the seams 5" to 7" apart. Backstitch at the beginning and end of each seam to secure.

Adding the Crinkle and Fringe Strips

The 4" x 35" strips can be used to make either crinkle or fringe accent strips on the outside of the tunnel in the area 8" below the hemmed rectangle edge. Please note that the strips do not extend completely across the rectangle.

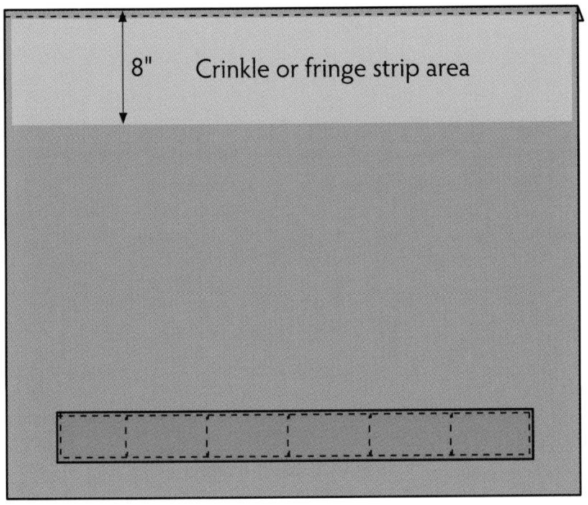

To add one crinkle and two fringe strips, as shown, follow these steps:

1. With right sides together, center and position the long edge of one print fringe strip 2" below the hemmed rectangle edge. Stitch through the center of the strip, parallel to the rectangle edge, to secure. Fold the unsewn strip edges toward the hemmed edge.

2. Fold the 4" crinkle strip in half lengthwise wrong sides together. Place the crinkle strip on top of the folded fringe strip, with the folded edge of the crinkle strip toward the hemmed rectangle edge, and the cut edges of the crinkle strip ½" from the seam of the fringe strip. Stitch the crinkle strip to the rectangle, ½" from the cut edges of the strip. Fold the strip toward the hemmed rectangle edge.

3. Place the remaining fringe strip right sides together with the rectangle, aligning one long edge with the folded edge of the crinkle strip. Sew down the center of the strip, parallel to the long edges, to secure.

4. Tape one end of the 10"-wide emergency-blanket strip to a large safety pin or bodkin and carefully thread the blanket strip through the crinkle strip channel. Trim off any excess blanket strip and sew the channel ends closed.

5. Fold the edges of one fringe strip away from the rest of the tunnel cover. Make multiple cuts ⅜" to ¼" apart and perpendicular to the long strip edge, to create the fringe. Repeat with the remaining fringe strip.

Finishing the Tunnel Toy

1. Fold the tunnel cover right sides together, matching the hemmed end and side edges. Stitch along the 35" side to form a tube.

2. Fold the hemmed edge of the tunnel cover 9" to the wrong side. Pin, and then stitch ½" from the folded edge to create a channel, or rib. Backstitch over the seam where it crosses the side seam from step 1. Repeat, folding the hemmed edge 14" to the wrong side. Pin, and then stitch ½" from the folded edge, creating a second channel.

3. Fold the unhemmed edge of the tunnel cover 7" to the wrong side. Pin, and then stitch ½" from the folded edge to make a third channel. Backstitch over the seam where it crosses the side seam from step 1.

4. Fold the 13"-wide emergency-blanket strip roughly in half, and hand tack the corners of the folded strip to one side of one batting piece. This will be the inside of the tunnel. Whipstitch the short ends of the batting piece together to form a tube.

5. Place the wrong side of the tunnel cover against the inside of the batting tube. Wrap the unhemmed edge of the tunnel cover over the outside of the tube. Pull the hemmed edge of the tunnel cover down over the top of the batting tube, covering the unhemmed edge. The first channel made in step 2 and the channel made in step 3 should be at the upper and lower outer edges of the tunnel. **Note:** The interior of the tunnel cover will not fit tightly against the batting.

6. If desired, cut the craft wire into two 45" lengths and insert them into the top and bottom channels to help keep the batting tube from collapsing. To insert the wires, bend a tight loop at one end of one wire. Snip the side seam stitches of the channel at the top of the tunnel, and insert the wire, loop end first, into the channel, curving the wire around the tunnel. Then bend a loop around the other end of the wire, and hook the loops together. Push the loops into the channel to hide the ends. Repeat to insert a wire into the channel at the base of the tunnel.

Just a Thought . . .

Get creative! Now that you have the general idea of how to make fringe and pockets, tailor your next tunnel cover to your individual cat's curiosities. As with any pet toy, remove the toy from use if it becomes too raggedy or worn.

Bonus Project

Make a fringe ball toy from the tunnel-cover remnants, following the instructions for making pom-poms on page 18.

Resources

As you begin your fleece-sewing adventure, you'll find a wide variety of notions and gadgets available to help you. Thanks to the companies that provided products used in this book.

AccuQuilt
www.accuquilt.com
Fabric cutters

Clover Needlecraft
www.clover-usa.com
Wonder Clips

Fairfield Processing Corp.
www.fairfieldworld.com
Poly-Fil Nu-Foam densified polyester
Poly-Fil stuffing

Fiskars
www.fiskars.com
Decorative rotary-cutter blades

June Tailor
www.junetailor.com
Fleece glue
Fringe Cut Express
Round the Corner ruler
Weave and Wave ruler

Nancy's Notions
www.nancysnotions.com
Edge Perfect Blade
Walking foot

Olfa
www.olfa.com
Decorative rotary-cutter blades

Prym Consumer USA
www.dritz.com
Wash Away Wonder Tape

Sizzix
www.sizzix.com
Big fabi personal fabric cutter

Sulky
www.sulky.com
Invisible polyester thread
KK2000 temporary spray adhesive

Tiger Tape
www.tigertape.com
Tiger Tape adhesive stitching guides

About the Contributors

Linda Turner Griepentrog is a writer, editor, and designer living in Bend, Oregon, with her husband, Keith (a long-arm quilter), and three dogs. In addition to her work with words, she also leads tours to Hong Kong for fabric lovers. Fleece is the daily uniform of Bendites year-round, even in the summer, with cold high-desert nighttime temps. Linda, former editor of *Sew News* magazine, is the author of six books, a contributor to many others, and author of thousands of articles for sewing, crafting, and quilting magazines.

Missy Shepler is an illustrator, author, and designer with a home-based studio in central Illinois. She learned to sew a long time ago by pushing a big needle threaded with thick yarn through prepunched sewing cards, and she hasn't stopped stitching yet. Missy has coauthored two books, contributed quilt designs and sewing patterns to many publications, and happily created more how-to illustrations than she can count. See her latest work online at MissyStitches.com.

Beth Bradley is a senior editor with Martingale, and she has loved fabric as long as she can remember. She made her first small quilt (with lots of help from her grandma) when she was eight, and was immediately hooked. She went on to earn a degree in apparel design and feels very lucky to have turned her fabric obsession into her livelihood, first as a clothing designer and now as an editor. She loves spending the day surrounded by beautiful quilts, inspiring books, and incredibly gifted artists.